RPET

A Survival Guide on
Keeping Up with the Hiltons

Celebra
Published by New American Library, a division of Penguin Group (USA) Inc., 375 Hudson Street, New York, New York 10014, USA • Penguin Group (Canada), 90 Eglinton Avenue East, Suite 700, Toronto, Ontario M4P 2Y3, Canada (a division of Pearson Penguin Canada Inc.) • Penguin Books Ltd., 80 Strand, London WC2R 0RL, England • Penguin Ireland, 25 St. Stephen's Green, Dublin 2, Ireland (a division of Penguin Books Ltd.) • Penguin Group (Australia), 250 Camberwell Road, Camberwell, Victoria 3124, Australia (a division of Pearson Australia Group Pty. Ltd.) • Penguin Books India Pvt. Ltd., 11 Community Centre, Panchsheel Park, New Delhi - 110 017, India • Penguin Group (NZ), 67 Apollo Drive, Rosedale, North Shore 0632, New Zealand (a division of Pearson New Zealand Ltd.) • Penguin Books (South Africa) (Pty.) Ltd., 24 Sturdee Avenue, Rosebank, Johannesburg 2196, South Africa

Penguin Books Ltd., Registered Offices:
80 Strand, London WC2R 0RL, England

First published by Celebra,
a division of Penguin Group (USA) Inc.

First Printing, January 2009
10 9 8 7 6 5 4 3 2 1

LIBRARY OF CONGRESS CATALOGING-IN-PUBLICATION DATA:

Hilton, Perez, 1978–
    Red carpet suicide: a survival guide on keeping up with the hiltons/Perez Hilton; with Jared Shapiro.
        p. cm.
    ISBN 978-0-451-22521-4
        1. Celebrities—Humor.   2. Celebrities—Miscellanea.   3. Hilton, Perez, 1978–   I. Shapiro, Jared.   II. Title.

PN6231.C25H55   2009
818'.6025—dc22   2008045110

Set in Serifa
Designed by Pauline Neuwirth, Neuwirth & Associates, Inc.

Printed in the United States of America

PUBLISHER'S NOTE
While the author has made every effort to provide accurate telephone numbers and Internet addresses at the time of publication, neither the publisher nor the author assumes any responsibility for errors, or for changes that occur after publication. Further, publisher does not have any control over and does not assume any responsibility for author or third-party Web sites or their content.

CoNTeNTs

This book is dedicated to
Britney Spears.

Many, many thanks to the millions of people worldwide who read my little Web site each day. None of this would be possible without you all and I can't genuinely express enough the magnitude of my appreciation. You have made my life better and you allow me into your homes on a daily basis. That's something truly special!

Thanks to Jared Shapiro for being my partner on this. Here's to many more!

Thanks to Scott Hoffman, Ray Garcia, Adrienne Avila, and everyone at Celebra for helping make my first book the huge success I hope (think) it will be.

Thanks to Todd Rubenstein, Andrew Meyer, Henry Copeland, Barbara Lavandeira, Milly Diaz, and all the amazing people on Team Perez. From this book to the clothing line and the radio deal, you've all helped me accomplish so much in 2008. To many more years of continued success!

Thanks to my dog, the adorable Teddy Hilton, for giving me lots of cuddles and kisses.

And I saved the best for last! Thanks to my mom for being the best. *Te quiero mucho!*

FOREWORD

by Andy Warhol

In 1968, I said, "In the future, everyone will be world-famous for fifteen minutes." This statement itself became so famous that everyone asked me about it all the time, and I grew very bored with repeating it. To make things lively, I began to confuse dull interviewers by switching it up. My first iteration was the mildly interesting "In the future, fifteen people will be famous." Naturally, I was thinking specifically of fifteen of my own protégés: Candy Darling, Penny Arcade, Mario Montez, Francis Francine, Holly Woodlawn, and you get the idea. But it was with my second mix-up that I accidentally stumbled on a gem of foresight: "In fifteen minutes, everybody will be famous." Which is to say, it is not the fame that will be limited to a few minutes, but rather the time it will take for fame to arrive. Today, you live in a world where in a millisecond, fame is achieved, linked, and permanently archived by

Google's fastidious Web-crawling Martian spiders. Fame lasts forever and happens instantly, to everyone.

It used to be that we all drank the same Coke. Whether you were the president or a bum on the corner, no amount of money or fame could get you a better Coke than the one everyone else had. Now we all have the same camera phones, camcorders, MySpace, Facebook, and YouTube. Like every celebrity before them, ordinary people couldn't trade their privacy fast enough for some measure of fame. Now your zodiac sign is as easy to Google as Lindsay Lohan's. Vanity is the new Coke, and it's more democratic than the vote. Why? Because you don't have to be eighteen to have a MySpace page. "Who's who" has become "who is."

Add to this mind-set a barrage of twenty-four-hour news programs, the explosion of reality television, celebrity magazines, and constantly updated news and gossip Web sites. The Earth has evolved into a breaking-news, gossip-hungry, minute-by-minute, click-to-refresh world. We're no longer a planet of people interested in gossip and breaking news; we're literally obsessed with finding out the next hot piece of dirt.

Enter Perez Hilton, the most important and influential person in all of media and entertainment. It's no exaggeration that once Perez writes about you, the whole world knows about it immediately. His praise can help you (Amy Winehouse, the Jonas Brothers, and Kylie Minogue would like to thank Perez!), and his criticism can destroy you (RIP, Tara Reid). If you're like Jessica "Don't Call Me Latina" Alba, and you are downplaying your ethnic heritage, Perez is going to call you on it. If you are FOX News host John Gibson and you make a tacky joke about

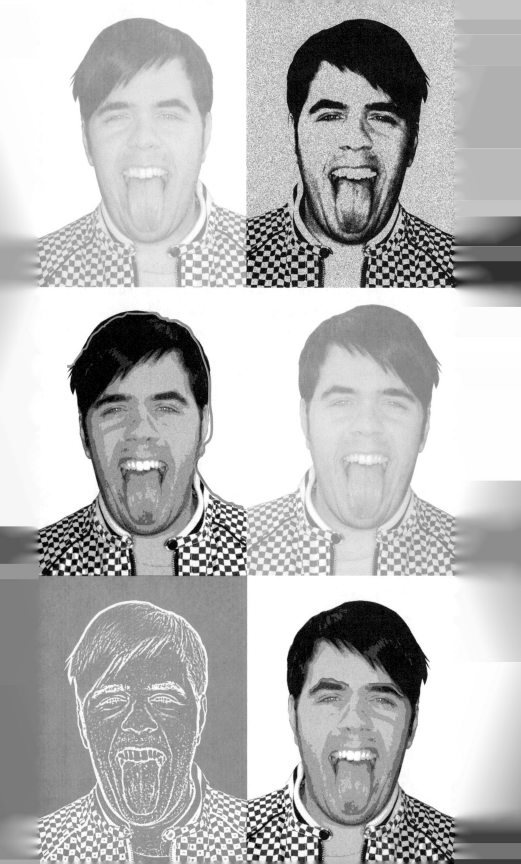

Heath Ledger's death, then don't be surprised when Perez posts your clip online for the whole world to criticize until you are stripped of your show. When Brad Pitt and Angelina were rumored to be seeing each other, there was very little evidence—until Perez Hilton posted the first shots of Brad and Angelina on the beach in Kenya. It crashed his site, but Brangelina was born.

If you're a "singer" and you make a horrible record, or if your movie bombs on opening weekend or just goes straight to DVD, or if you launch a boring advertising campaign for a lame product, Perez will call you out. Before an audience of millions, he will draw an MS Paint penis on your face—plus some coke falling out of your nose and the word *whoreanus* across your forehead. Then you will hear the scurrying clatter of a million robot spiders sent by Google to collect, catalog, and archive your shame for all eternity.

Even I didn't see it coming to this.

A.W.

Heaven, 2009

INTRODUCTION

Hello, bitches! Perez Hilton, the Queen of All Media, here!

I wouldn't be a self-proclaimed Hilton without penning a book of my own, now, would I? After all, I went through my own rite of passage and gained access to the crazy, sensational celebrity world. But I thought to myself, "Why should I have all the fun?" Like Paris, I'd like to make this world a hotter place. So this book, my friends, was written for you. In these pages, I'll show you what it takes to reach celebrity status, and how, with a few wobbly steps and a case of Astroglide, you too can be a hilton! I don't mean that you should be a street-corner whore (but you're definitely getting warmer!). No, what I mean is, you can live like the rich, famous, and utterly depraved without even an ounce of talent or dignity.

Tired Reid is a good example of a hilton success story. I can't even remember the last real work she's done. After all those horrible movies, train-wreck media appearances, and documented drunken partying, you'd think she'd be banned from Hollywood forever. But somehow she still finds her way into magazines and is even popular in Australia! How can someone who's made suicide moves to her "career"—on the red carpet, no less—still get attention? It's because she belongs to the Hilton generation of Hollywood, and for these hiltons, scandalous behavior is actually not a suicide attempt at all. In fact, a red carpet suicide, a disastrous celebrity moment that would normally be seen as the end of a Hollywood career, is actually a hilton's claim to fame. Clearly, the Hilton generation has taken over Hollywood and has rewritten the rules.

But what and who, you ask, is a hilton, and why does it seem that everyone in Hollywood wants to be one? Well, it all stems from this country's obsession with celebrities and how our culture is driven by them. When celebrities go green, we stop drinking bottled water and start composting in our studio apartments. They tell us to sneak pureed carrots into brownies, and suddenly our kids are reading past lights-out. When they study the kabbalah and yoga, we become mystical pretzels. Since the beginning of Hollywood, celebrities have ruled the world, and it doesn't seem like that aspect will change. Although what has changed (and just recently) is the image of the celebrity. These days, fame is no longer limited to the actress on the red carpet, the rock star packing the arena, or the athlete tearing up the megadome. These untouchable, elusive, and private celebrities are all being eclipsed by another kind of star.

Now we have hiltons people: we confuse with celebrities. No one even knows how they became famous or, more accurately, how they became famous for being famous. You see, a hilton is someone who is skinny, notorious, mischievous, hot, loves to party, dates a lot, acts gorgeous, drives drunk, poses seductively for the camera, rarely works, dates some more, and doesn't eat. They appear on reality TV and in bad movies, but they can't act; they make records, but they can't sing or play the keytar; their athletic prowess is limited to bedroom gymnastics; and somehow, they are the hottest names in entertainment. Today, reality television stars are gracing more covers than actual actors, and famous sluts are signing on with music labels and designers, when truly talented folks can't even get a decent rejection letter for their vocals or designs. Hiltons lack any real talent, so they have to resort to using scandal and debauchery to catapult them to fame and celebrity status.

> a hilton is someone who is skinny, notorious, mischievous, hot, loves to party, dates a lot, acts gorgeous, drives drunk, poses seductively for the camera, rarely works, dates some more, and doesn't eat.

The result of all of this is that right now, everyone in Hollywood has the same checklist, and they're all desperately trying to be a hilton. Talented artists are watching spoiled bitches get more famous than they are, and they feel like they need to jump on the bandwagon. They want to know, Why can't *we* hoard all the attention, without the dull business of meriting any?

And how is this Hilton generation affecting the real celebrities, those actors, musicians, and athletes who are recognized for actual talent? Well, we still admire them for their work, but they are not nearly as addicting to watch. They definitely shouldn't be confused with hiltons, but there are those few who are just over-the-top and plain crazy (like Tom Cruise jumping on Oprah's couch, or Michael Jackson waving his child over a balcony) and exhibit hilton behavior. They're easily put on the wall of shame because it's shocking to see these folks resort to or caught doing hilton antics. It's even juicier because of this. And negative attention is good for publicity in this Hollywood era, so it doesn't really matter what they do. They are still on our radar. (Just so we don't raise any confusion, when I refer to real celebs as "hiltons," I'm merely describing the shocking behavior they are caught doing or shamelessly exhibiting. Because the real essence of a hilton is the scandal that's associated with him or her.)

All of Hollywood embraces and profits from the rules of this Hilton generation, and everyone who wants in needs to start thinking like a hilton. People think you just have to show up to an event, act famous, and then everyone will love you. Wrong. They have to hate you to love you. I know that part very well. They have to love talking about you, but hate the fact that they love it. To be a hilton, you have to love to be hated, or at least not care if you are hated. A hilton has to think of creative ways to hoard attention—it's not enough to have your publicist tip off the paparazzi that you'll be shopping at Intuition; you've got to get caught for possession a week after your sex tape leaks out. Hiltons aren't elusive or mysterious; they don't know the meaning of "that's private." A hilton is someone with little talent who doesn't seem smart, but they sure know how to make money and a career out of acting like they're hotter and better than everyone else.

Sounds easy enough, right? Wrong. True, it doesn't take much brains—just big boobs and a photogenic vagina—to set your hilton path. But what it *does* take is a tremendous amount of work and sacrifice to earn the title. Some people spend *years* whoring themselves to the media just to get their fifteen minutes of fame. Time is money, bitches, so it's wise to have an efficient strategy and know how to play within the rules of Hollywood.

Being a player in the gossip game has given me an insider's view of fame, celebrity, and scandal. I've been doing this for many years now, and, lucky for you, I'm going to share with you in the following pages all of my knowledge in a how-to format—because to quote Jessica Simpson, there are no such things as applied sciences, only applications of science. In fact, consider this book your bible to fame whoredom. All it really takes is a few red carpet suicides to make it in Hollywood, and I've handpicked the twelve most effective ones and presented them to you in twelve easy steps. If you follow them like the Ten Commandments, you too will enter the kingdom of Hollywood and reap the rewards: premieres, bottle service, late-night parties, hard-core sex, big money, fast cars, and tabloid cover stories.

You can find these twelve red carpet suicides in the first part of this book, "Becoming a Hilton." After you've made your media-whore transformation, proceed to the second part of the book, "The Future of Hilton," where you will learn how the Hilton generation will evolve and who will be the next set of celebrities to rule Hollywood. Who knows, maybe your name will be included in that list after reading this book! And finally, the third part, "My Life as a Hilton," documents my own journey through Hollywood and hilton life. I'll let you in on some of my juicy celebrity secrets and outrageous encounters!

But before you even start reading the first part of this book, you should get to know the hilton types, so you know which one you want to be and whom you want to model your suicide attempts from. The following are token hiltons to consider. Mix and match. Be creative and make a hilton mutant even! There are no limits when you are a hilton.

★

The Heiress: This hilton's fame is truly in the name, so if you were born an heiress, most of the work is already done for you. If you're not as lucky, make up a name and fake the funk. And make sure you have your princess image down to a T!

EXAMPLES: Paris Hilton, Nicole Richie, Brooke Hogan, Kelly Osbourne, Drew Barrymore, Tori Spelling

IDENTIFYING QUOTE: "Daddy, I want an Oompa-Loompa *now!*"

★

The Sibling: This hilton thrives on the demise of his or her famous sibling(s). They're like scavengers who pick up the scraps—though you might need to do some waiting around and real sacrificing if you want to follow in this hilton's footsteps. La Toya Jackson has to wait for Michael to have another boys-only sleepover before she outs him to the media or publicly admonishes him for his behavior. And then there's Ashlee Simpson, who wanted to be just like Jessica, and did just that when she got a nose job!

EXAMPLES: Ashlee Simpson, Ali Lohan, Aaron Carter, Jamie Lynn Spears

IDENTIFYING QUOTE: "Marcia, Marcia, Marcia!"

The Reality Star: The best part about this hilton is that all you need is to be yourself. Except more annoying! Though it's definitely the easiest way to get fame, it also has the shortest shelf life. In no time, Lauren Conrad will be long forgotten and won't be able to find anyone who'll want her, except maybe *Hollywood Squares*. Even then, we won't be able to remember why she was famous.

EXAMPLES: Lauren Conrad, Spencer Pratt, Kim Kardashian, Tila Tequila

IDENTIFYING QUOTE: "How can you possibly not know who I am?"

★

The Has-been: These hiltons just can't accept their faded spotlight and do whatever they can to stay in the game. They'll do anything and anyone to keep their platform, and sometimes it pays off. Some of these hiltons still end up in magazines, but only for filler purposes.

EXAMPLES: Tara Reid, Nick Carter, Nick Lachey, Mischa Barton

IDENTIFYING QUOTE: "Find me a script . . . or a scandal!"

★

The Disney Sexpot: This hilton is a whore in training and has a pretty influential pimp: Disney. Try out to be the next Hannah Montana and just play into the media's expectations. It's this hilton's destiny to be the slut of Hollywood.

EXAMPLES: Lindsay Lohan, Miley Cyrus, Britney Spears, Christina Aguilera, Vanessa Hudgens

IDENTIFYING QUOTE: "Have you ever kissed a mouse between the ears? Would you like to?"

So now that you know your hilton type, you're ready to get started! And for those who are worried that you might not have the talent to make it, just remember that it doesn't take any talent at all! With just a little help from a drug dealer and the local liquor store, anyone can be a hilton and rule the world. Even you!

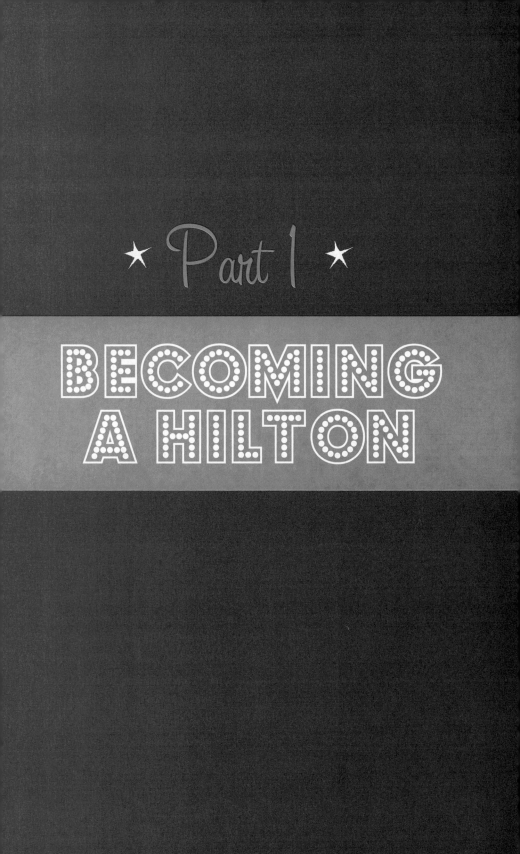

Part 1

BECOMING A HILTON

EAT!

BE A SKINNY BITCH

A hilton can never be too skinny. That's why celebrities don't buy dinner; they rent it! Just minutes later, they're giving it back to the community (or at least to the sewer alligators).

The next time you are in one of the big celebrity cities, go to a fancy restaurant (may I suggest Madeo, Il Sole, or CUT in LA? The Pump Room in Chicago? Nobu or Kobe Club in NYC?) and have a seat in one of the bathroom stalls from eight to eleven p.m. Tell me how many ralphing sessions you hear. I'm betting on at least two or three. And that's just the "regular" people—because celebrities wouldn't dare expose themselves like that in public. There's always a hidden camera somewhere! (Right, Lindsay?)

Don't believe me? What would you say if I told you that I have actually heard the sounds on numerous occasions? Anyone who's been out to dinner at these trendy spots has heard the heaving noises coming from the bathrooms. I knew a handyman who told me that the pipes in LA are eroding from all the stomach acid!

be a gym rat

Women like Jessica Biel and Kate Hudson can eat anything they want without barfing it back up. They are young, and you can tell they work out like crazy. Kate Hudson admitted to working out three hours a day for three months to lose her pregnancy weight, and every day, a pregnant Jessica Alba went to and from the gym. Vanessa Hudgens knows she's not as pretty as Zacquisha, so there she goes, walking to the gym, water bottle in hand. Their bodies are ripped. Nicole Kidman was, like, six months preggers before her baby bump even started showing. Mario Lopez wrote a book just about his abs (no more burgers at the Max for him!). Who the hell has time to do a thousand sit-ups a day? Mario Lopez, obviously! They'll have the pizza. But you won't!

Janet Jackson's dramatic weight loss success landed her the highest selling issue of *Us Weekly* at that time.

PEREZ FACT

THE KATE HUDSON SEX WORKOUT

She breaks up with Owen, she gets back together with him, she breaks up with him again, she hooks up with Lance Armstrong. . . . Hooking up with Lance Armstrong? That guy can go for twenty-three days straight! He's the Tour de France champ! She obviously loves to sweat, and now we know how she stays so skinny. Maybe she was tired of looking fat next to Chris Robinson, her pin-thin ex-hubby?

Hiltons get paid to look good, and spend hours a day making themselves look good. The rest of us get paid to book hotel reservations or collect bridge tolls. But not for long! And unless you are so lucky as to a) be young, and b) have the time, money, and willpower for personal training *ten times per week,* you *cannot* mimic their results without the additional help of an eating disorder.

be scary skinny

When she was pulled over for a DUI in December 2006, the five-foot-one Nicole Richie weighed eighty-five pounds. But she didn't get arrested for being too skinny, because there's no law against weighing eighty-five pounds. I've got to think that if she didn't get pulled over then, she could have totally pushed it to eighty pounds by January! Think how hot her clavicle

When I met Posh, I offered her a cookie and she wouldn't eat it, not even for the cameras (she was taping her ill-fated reality show). That's the kind of dedication you need!

PEREZ NOTE

A Hilton Diet

water   diet pills   air

carbs

and bony arms would have looked, and how delicate her zombie hands would have been. Her child-size dresses would have been clinging to her bones just like on a department store hanger, and we all know how good dresses look on the hanger.

Ever heard of the Master Cleanse? I did it for a while. It's like a fast—literally a diet consisting of honey, water, and cayenne pepper. Beyoncé and Jared Leto have both admitted to using it. Some hiltons use the IV diet, where you check into the hospital and get hooked up to an IV, and you don't eat at all. None of this is "part of a complete breakfast" or "a sensible dinner." A hilton knows only "part of a complete fast" and "an insensible dinner." While everyone else is on the Atkins, South Beach, or Zone diet, a hilton is on the Air diet: some water, several diet pills, a ton of air. Easy to remember!

For normal people, being too skinny can harm you. (Everyone will gossip about you at parties! People will point and you will become the object of insults and jokes!) But if you're a hilton, being too skinny works to your advantage. (Everyone will gossip about you at parties! People will point and you will become the object of insults and jokes!)

The old saying that the camera adds fifteen pounds couldn't
be more true. It's shocking how
skinny hiltons are in person. It's
borderline disgusting. If you're
not from LA, it's almost worth
taking a trip to come see the freaks!
When I tell you they are skinny, you
really have no idea until they walk up
next to you at the Coffee Bean and order
a sugar-free skim latte. That's when you see—
with your own eyes—that skinny don't look so good
in person. But who cares about how you look in person, in your
actual life? The camera is what's important, real, and forever.

> But who cares about how you look in person, in your actual life? The camera is what's important, real, and forever.

learn the real poop on skinny

So how *does* a hilton get so skinny so quickly? On top of being
the world's largest vomitorium, Hollywood is also its largest phar-
macy, stocked with laxatives, metabolizers, herbs, pills, elixirs,
and drugs. Hiltons resort to suppositories, diet pills, and internal
cleansers like SoCal Cleanse. They get enemas and colonics.
The calories have to go, and if they're not coming out one end,
the other end will do. Princess Di reportedly spent over $4,300
a year on colonics. Damon Wayans, Janet Jackson, Ben Affleck,
Courtney Love, Andie MacDowell, Usher, Cindy Crawford, Gwen
Stefani, Gisele Bündchen, Alicia Silverstone, and Liv Tyler have
all gone to colonic centers, and John Lennon, James Coburn,
and Mae West all swore by it back when it was called hydro-
therapy. Remember when Dave Navarro and Carmen Electra
went together on their reality show *'Til Death Do Us Part* and got

a "couples colonic" together? That's so romantic, who could have predicted their relationship would soon go to shit?

I got a colonic once. They stick a warm tube in you and flush out your insides. They lay you down on your side, massage your stomach for a minute, and then bam! Out comes a grape Now and Later from seventh grade. That was the last time I tried that!

Yuk

choose your diet plan

Don't be fooled by these celebrities who say that they eat whatever they want, whenever they want. That's a lie. They starve themselves, they work out like crazy, and they spend all of their time and energy on "fitness" (eating disorders). And that's what you're going to do! Now, I can't help myself here, so let's be clear on the fact that hilton diet plans are not executed successfully through sheer willpower alone. Everyone needs a little help, not to mention a little energy, which is something non-hiltons get from food. A hilton needs a little pick-me-up. Lindsay Lohan was in the presence of cocaine both times she was arrested for DUI; meanwhile, Nicole Richie's arresting officers found heroin in her car. It's also been said that Paris, Britney, Lindsay, and Nicole are all fans of Adderall, which made a special guest appearance at some arrests. All three drugs—cocaine, heroin, and Adderall—are well-known for making your weight go down faster than a "model/actress" in a private audition. So with all of that in mind, consider my favorite diet plans:

Lindsay's "Booger Sugar" Diet:

The trick to LiLo's svelte bod is the use of certain *ingredients* that speed up the metabolism. Strawberry Quik isn't what it used to be, though you'll still need a straw. (And you thought that rabbit had impulse-control issues before!)

Breakfast
Sugar-free skim latte

Lunch
Cigarettes
Svedka vodka

Dinner
Strawberry Quik
Mescaline salad
Snow cones
Brown sugar

PRO TIP: Lindsay occasionally tries a diet of cold turkey.

★

Oprah's Yo-yo Diet:

A gentle and wise soul once said if you want to look skinny, stand next to a fat cow. As she has done with everything in her life, Oprah took this advice to the next level. She realized that the best way to look skinny is to *be* the fat cow (Zen!), *then* lose the weight. What a contrast! Then, if people stop complimenting you, put the weight back on! Don't let them get complacent. Wait for their expectations to finally bottom out, then lose the weight again. You can't have sunshine without rain, and you can't have "dramatic weight loss" without "dramatic weight."

Day 1

Breakfast:

1 granola bar

Lunch:

1 potato chip

Dinner:

1 positive affirmation

Day 2

Breakfast:

Your daily slice, cut it thin and toast it twice

Lunch:

4 oz. poached chicken (boneless, skinless, joyless)
1 head broccoli, steamed (hunger is the best sauce)

Dinner:

Two Lean Cuisines
1 pint fat-free frozen yogurt
3 potato chips

Day 3

Breakfast:

2 gallons Ben & Jerry's Chubby Hubby

Lunch:

20,000 potato chips

Dinner:

All of Dr. Oz's "what not to eat" food list

EXERCISE TIP: Run like Stedman's chasing you for sex.

★

Kate Bosworth's Diet: What? Are you waiting for something?

★

Tara Reid's Liquid Diet: Imagine a crowd of horny frat boys chanting, "Chug! Chug! Chug! Chug!" This is your diet support group. Beer has barley, wheat, corn, and rice, and it's a great source of semen (eventually)—all part of your complete breakfast. And since liquid breaks down so much quicker than solids, it's basically perfect. If you find that you're still hungry, try these:

water

vodka

Breakfast
Celery from Bloody Marys

Lunch
Lime wedges from Coronas

Dinner
Martini olives

PRO TIP: Order a Manhattan for a cherry dessert.

★

Elizabeth Hurley Diet: This is how she claims she lost the baby weight after the birth of her son, Damian.

For each meal, choose one of the following (*one*, cow!):
A banana
Six raisins

★

Amy Winehouse's Toxic Diet: Calories will leak out of your open sores, and you will also lose the unwanted weight of your teeth.

For breakfast, lunch, and dinner, combine well:

2 parts Drano

2 parts Clorox

1 part kitty litter

1/2 part hair spray

Draw into a syringe and inject into your eyeball.

★

The Samantha Ronson Diet: Keeping a boyish figure is important when you are the lamprey to Lindsay Lohan's shark. It's not enough to know that SaMANtha likes to dine at the Y; it's just as important to know her menu preferences:

Tuna taco

Bearded clam

Roast beef sandwich

Fur burger

Hair pie

Sausage wallet

Whisker biscuit

Box lunch

Fish dinner

★

Marcia Cross's Baby Food Diet: You rarely see a baby over twenty or thirty pounds, and you've probably wondered how they do it. Baby food is how they do it, and taking it from them is easier than stealing Jane Mancini's husband.

Breakfast

1 jar Prunes & Oatmeal

Lunch

1 jar Vegetables, Turkey & Barley

Dinner

1 baby (first remove your wig in front of a mirror to expose the gruesome scar left by Michael's drunken car crash)

★

The Jennifer Love Hewitt Diet: Jennifer Love Handles outlined this menu for *Every Day with Rachael Ray* magazine, and it's perfect for anyone who wants to appear on the cover of *People* with the caption, "Stop Calling Me Fat!"

Breakfast

2 biscuits with honey

1 cup tea

Lunch

1 bowl chicken couscous with peppers, onions, and mushrooms

1 bottle water

Dinner

- 1 strawberry-banana shake
- 1 scoop tuna salad
- 1 bowl soup
- 1 apple
- 1 Sprite

Dessert

- 1 heaping scoop of sweet denial

★

The Katie Holmes Diet: Katie has been morphing into Posh, getting her hair cut the same way and following Victoria's stern nine-hundred-calories-per-day eating plan.

For breakfast, lunch, and dinner:
- 1 seaweed shake
- 1 cup frozen grapes
- 1 cup edamame

Why isn't this plan called the Victoria Beckham diet? Because Posh would never eat nine hundred calories in one day; that's for cows like Katie Holmes!

> **They starve themselves, they work out like crazy, and they spend all of their time and energy on "fitness" (eating disorders).**

★

The Knightley Family Ancestral Diet: Even though *anorexia* is the first word that comes to mind when I hear Keira Knightley's name, she denies that she suffers from it, and she even sued a British tabloid for

Scary Skinny! Pin Thin!

implying she has the disorder. Somewhat insanely, she claims her grandmother and great-grandmother suffered from the disease. So great-grandmother Knightley refused to eat in, like, the year 1895?

For each meal:

Refuse your ration of mead, venison, and oats.

ONE TO GROWN ON:

Did you know there was an extraskinny supermodel in the 1960s named Twiggy? She was one of a kind—hence the name "Twiggy." Nowadays, eating disorders have become so common in Hollywood that we're immune to them. We don't call Nicole Richie "Twiggy," even though she's skinnier than Twiggy ever was. We just call her "Nicole."

The Ellen Pompeo Diet: Oh, who the fuck cares about Ellen Pompeo?

put on a faux food show

You'll want to join the new trend that hiltons are putting over on the American public: the Faux Food Show. It's when celebrities show off how much they *love* regular food. And by regular food, I mean fast-food restaurants where you can see them in clear view enjoying a giant burger, fries, and soda.

You never go into Olive Garden, Red Lobster, Applebee's, or (my all-time fave) T.G.I. Fridays! These places are completely enclosed and covered. Hiltons could never be photographed eating there, because it's too dark, and you can't get shots from far away. But Fatburger—now, that has wide-open, giant storefront windows for the paparazzi to look right into and get a few good hundred photos that scream, "Look at me! I love burgers! I'm not anorexic!"

"Look, there's Nicole Richie eating a giant double-decker triple cheeseburger with fries and gravy on top!" *Snap, click*—and then the caption in the magazine reads, "Finally She Eats!" What you don't see is where the burger ends up a few minutes later, tasting almost as good as it did the first time.

Nicole Richie

Before eating

After eating

Puke

Paris Hilton, Lindsay Lohan, Nicole Richie, and even Hilary Swank (on Oscar night in her gown!) have been spotted doing the Faux Food Show. In fact, Nicole turned it into an art form. At one point, she was having fast food delivered to her at the clubs so she could "eat" it in front of everyone! I can't even imagine a nonanorexic doing that.

Nonanorexics eat Wendy's in their cars like feral dogs, hiding from shame and scavengers. That's how Kirstie Alley did it until she was caught on film, just weeks before landing a major endorsement deal with weight-loss guru Jenny Craig. Hmm . . . was that a *faux* Faux Food Show? Well played, Alley, well played.

skinny gets you attention

No, not just cute guys—though that is nothing to complain about. I mean the attention that matters: magazine editors! When's the last time anyone cared about Jennifer Love Hewitt? Yet she landed the cover of *People* by declaring she wasn't fat (even though she was!). Was Tori Spelling ever fat? I mean, she was pregnant, so, yeah, she put on some weight, but eventually eight pounds of it would come right out of her vagina. But now, anytime she's in a magazine, she's talking about her diet or her weight. Ricki Lake is on the cover of countless magazines, but what did that girl ever do in the past ten years? She lost weight! Woo-hoo! From, like, 2000 to 2005, it was all about Kirstie Alley—but, oops, she couldn't keep the weight off. Then it became Valerie Bertinelli. Throw Queen Latifah in there, too. But name me one successful project—besides Queen Latifah's *Chicago* in 2002—that any of these people really had going on? Tori had her reality show, *Tori & Dean: Inn Love,* but do you think an Oxygen

Network reality show would have gotten her magazine covers? Lucky for her, America is obsessed with weight.

get your fat ass off the fence

If you're still on the fence about becoming scary skinny, let me lay down my trump card. Remember 2000, when Nicole was Lionel Richie's sort-of daughter? A couple of years later, she had graduated to being Paris Hilton's cute, chubby sidekick. Then she got cast alongside Paris in a FOX reality show called *The Simple Life,* where she and the heiress brought jet-setter high jinks to middle America. That was it. She was semifamous for being on a small reality show on what was, at the time, the fourth-rated network.

Then she started to get skinny—fast. Season by season, she shrank. The pounds were dropping faster than the ratings of their show. Only then did she start landing on the covers of fashion magazines. Never before that. She got so skinny so publicly that you could literally chart her weight loss by way of the alarming headlines of weekly gossip magazines.

Remember that famous shot of Nicole and Lindsay Lohan going out on the town together in 2005? The two bony starlets were on the cover of *Star* magazine, and the headline read, "SCARY SKINNY!" It showed Lindsay at 112 pounds and Nicole at what they claimed to be a whopping 97 pounds (we now know the real numbers were even lower). They were inseparable that summer, two completely skeletal waifs going out on the town together to show off their bodies. They were like unholy Doublemint Twins, peddling anorexia instead of delicious gum. It was disgusting, but it landed them on the cover of every tabloid out there, and they knew exactly what they were doing.

Make no mistake about it, and let it be said officially now: Nicole Richie is famous solely because she got scary skinny. That's it.

Skinny has always been desired, especially in Hollywood, but it was never a game of chicken or a suicide competition. Not until Nicole got famous for it. Then everyone saw it for the bargain it could be: The closer you came to risking your mortal life, the more secure your immortal fame. I'm ready to sign that deal, aren't you?

> The closer you came to risking your mortal life, the more secure your immortal fame.

MEET JACK DANIEL'S, YOUR DESIGNATED DRIVER

Hollywood loves to tell you how much they party, and party means drink! And drink means shots, because a shot has a thousand times fewer calories than chugging beer. George Clooney is the voice of Budweiser commercials—but he's only

drinking the stuff when the camera is on him. I think Nick Lachey is the only person in Hollywood who actually drinks beer, and it shows (bitch tits). Hiltons have sugar-free Red Bull and vodka, vodka and soda with lime, and vodka and Diet Coke.

Once you're good and sauced, it's time to get some scandalous press. Drinking and driving is by far the easiest way to become notorious in Hollywood, and it's one of the easiest ways to become a hilton. These bitches are so eager to get a DUI, they must have confused it with a form of birth control.

What they don't seem to realize is that it's a great way to get yourself killed. That's because they didn't get the "don't drink

Test Your Skill

On the list below, check the names of those who have been cited for DUI:

- ☐ George Bush
- ☐ Dick Cheney
- ☐ Michelle Rodriguez
- ☐ Mischa Barton
- ☐ Mel Gibson
- ☐ Lindsay Lohan
- ☐ Nicole Richie
- ☐ Paris Hilton
- ☐ Ray Liotta
- ☐ Scott Weiland
- ☐ Kiefer Sutherland
- ☐ Vivica Fox

- ☐ Mickey Rourke
- ☐ Lane Garrison
- ☐ Eve
- ☐ Ty Pennington
- ☐ Busta Rhymes
- ☐ George Michael
- ☐ Rebecca De Mornay
- ☐ Richie Sambora
- ☐ Tracy Morgan
- ☐ Shemar Moore
- ☐ Jason Wahler
- ☐ Tim Allen

- ☐ Haley Joel Osment
- ☐ Thomas Jane
- ☐ Wynonna Judd
- ☐ Rip Torn
- ☐ Tracey Gold
- ☐ Nick Carter
- ☐ Andy Dick
- ☐ Mike Tyson
- ☐ Gus Van Sant
- ☐ Keanu Reeves

Answer Key: 1, 2, 3, 4, 5, 6, 7, 8, 9, 10, 11, 12, 13, 14, 15, 16, 17, 18, 19, 20, 21, 22, 23, 24, 25, 26, 27, 28, 29, 30, 31, 32, 33, 34.

and drive" talk from their parents, just like they didn't get the "wear underpants" talk. "Keep singing, Britney! Ten thousand dollars . . . twenty thousand . . . thirty thousand . . . Pay me, baby, one more time! Forty thousand . . . fifty thousand! *Cha-ching!*"

Do you really think that Lindsay's mom, the Orange Oprah, actually sat young LiLo down one day and said, "Now, Lindsay, now that we've talked about leaving a little hair 'down there,' let's talk about alcohol and driving." No, you don't. Because that did not happen.

Drinking and driving is by far the easiest way to become notorious in Hollywood, and it's one of the easiest ways to become a hilton.

The average American would love to be able to go out and get hammered and then have a black Escalade waiting for them out front to take them home or to the next bar, which is something every hilton can have. I've never understood celebrities who run up tabs in the thousands but don't seem to have money for a driver, or even cab fare.

give a fierce mug shot

In the real world, a DUI can ruin your reputation, if not your whole life. Your license gets suspended or you spend six months in jail. But in the alternate reality of the hiltons, a DUI is a surefire way to get famous, especially now that so many have made it cool. And it doesn't matter whether you are young and hot, like Mischa Barton, or old and batshit crazy, like Mel Gibson—if you drink and drive in Hollywood, you will get busted (read: attention!). The cops in LA are always looking for

PEREZ NOTE

the ultimate "get"—the pretty, rich, or famous. Hell, the paparazzi might even catch up to the situation and the arresting officer could end up in *Star* magazine!

Getting caught by the police and ending up all over PerezHilton.com, *Access Hollywood,* and FOX News is practically as good as getting your own show. If you think about it, the night Mischa was featured on *Access Hollywood* for her DUI, more people probably saw her there than actually watched her last season of *The O.C.*! It was the first dramatic role she played convincingly.

WORST THREE THINGS TO SAY DURING YOUR DUI ARREST

#3:
"I took Vicodin and pot."
—Nicole Richie

#2:
"Just put a gun to my head and shoot me!"
—Michelle Rodriguez

#1:
"Are you a Jew?"
—Mel Gibson

It was also her biggest hit in terms of ratings, and not just the TV coverage. For at least a few days, Mischa Barton was the

a DUI is a surefire way to get famous.

true Queen of All Media, and I don't share that title willingly. Within minutes of Mischa's year-ending 2007 drunk-driving case, her Breathalyzer statistics and mug shot were all across the Web and newspapers. And hers was one of the hottest mug shots in history by far.

pick the right dui for you

If you want to be a hilton, I can't overstate the importance of choosing the details of your DUIs carefully. You can't get too many without consequences, even as a hilton, so make each one count—they are a reflection of *you*! You can come up with your own, or add a personal twist to any one of these classics.

"The Mischa": Get hammered all night, then around two forty-five a.m., straddle two lanes of traffic and turn without signaling. Make sure you're doing all of this without a valid license. It would also be a nice touch to be listening to Whitestarr and thinking about Cisco's balls.

"The Lindsay": Start by going to rehab for drug and alcohol problems; then go out while wearing a court-ordered anklet that monitors blood-alcohol levels. Then less than two weeks later, get in a high-speed car chase along the PCH. Then get yourself a nice blood-alcohol level of .12 to .13, while the cops book you for suspicion of cocaine possession. Meanwhile, wonder where your

mom, the Orange Oprah, is during all of this, and realize she's probably pimping out her other daughter. "Ten thousand dollars . . . twenty thousand! Sing it, Ali! Thirty thousand . . . forty thousand . . . *Cha-ching!*"

"The Nicole": This move is very difficult and dangerous, because it involves GOING THE WRONG DIRECTION ON A MAJOR HIGHWAY! Do not try this unless you are simply desperate for publicity, and if you do, for the love of God, make sure you are in a large, German-made SUV, like Nicole was. After going the wrong way for a while, turn around and get back on the highway in the right direction. Stop in the middle of the carpool lane, put your foot on the brake, and call someone on your cell phone. (Maybe she ordered a pizza? Oh, wait, it's Nicole. Maybe she ordered some ice chips?) When the officers arrive, tell them you have just taken a few Vicodins and smoked some weed and are dancing on the ceiling!

"The Lane Garrison": I don't recommend the Lane Garrison. First, he killed someone. Second, he went to jail. Lane Garrison is the epitome of all that can go wrong. These little pop princesses get pulled over with no harm done, and we laugh and point fingers. But Lane Garrison actually killed someone. So never mind the Lane Garrison.

"The Gibson": We've all said some pretty stupid things while drunk, me especially! But Mel showed the world how to take it to the next level. When he was pulled over in 2006, a drunk Gibson shouted, "Fucking Jews . . . The Jews are responsible for all the wars in the world." Then he got an even better idea: Why not make this personal with the cops? After claiming to own all of Malibu, he called a female officer "sugar tits" and asked another officer,

I can't overstate the importance of choosing the details of your DUIs carefully.

"Are *you* a Jew?" What was Mel's angle here? Was he distracting the media from his DUI with anti-Semitism? Was he distracting from his anti-Semitism with a DUI? Was he trying to get a publicity explosion with a "twofer"? Wish granted! (In a little twist of irony, the drink called the Gibson was supposedly created by an investment banker who wanted his martini glass filled with water instead of gin, with a cocktail onion to distinguish his drink from the alcoholic ones—he wanted an advantage over his drunk clients. Gibson should have had a Gibson!)

"The Mickey Rourke": Get pulled over while driving a Vespa! Ha! BEST. DUI. EVER. He made an illegal U-turn, drunk, with a hot date grabbing onto him. Have you seen him lately? He should've been arrested for ruining his face.

"The Kiefer Sutherland": Get arrested for DUI and carrying a concealed and loaded weapon. Oh, don't act so surprised; everyone knows Jack Bauer sleeps with a pillow under his gun.

"Tha Busta Rhymes": Fail your sobriety test after being pulled over for "excessively tinted windows." Don't you hate when that happens? You tint your windows to have a low profile, but it just draws that much more attention to you! My favorite part about rappers getting pulled

over for DUI is that you get to find out their real names: Trevor Smith?!

"The Andy Dick": Get hammered and crash your car into a telephone pole. Then flee the scene on foot, only to be tackled by a witness (sounds more like "Andy Pussy"). Then watch as police search your car, where they find your stash of cocaine and marijuana.

"The George Bush": Get charged with "operating under the influence of an intoxicating liquor." Can you believe they still talked like that in 1976? Was he written up by the constable? Then again, this was in Maine, so they had probably just updated it from "Were it wyn, or oold or moysty ale, that he hath dronke, he hath also to do moore than ynough to kepen hym and his capul out of slough."

"The Haley Joel Osment": Let everyone know how tough times are for you, not because you are getting booked for DUI and pot possession, but because you're doing it in a 1995 Saturn! As a bonus, colliding with a brick pillar and flipping your car is a great way to "see dead people."

"The Paris": Have "one drink," get behind the wheel, and drive home. Paris said she had one margarita at a party. Who hasn't done that? Of course, what she didn't tell you is what else she had in her system. What she *also* didn't tell you is that I was at the party that night, and that math was never her strongest subject. Her blood-alcohol level was right at the minimum, but it was enough

to get her booked. Coincidentally, she had released her first CD just one week prior (I'm sure her record company was devastated by the publicity). Her response? "I was just really hungry and I wanted to have an In-N-Out Burger." In typical Paris fashion, she forgot that she was the pitchwoman for Carl's Jr. (who were no doubt hoping to be as devastated as her record company).

"The George Michael": If the other DUIs sound suicidal, it's because they are. You might be more comfortable with the George Michael: You just fall asleep behind a parked car.

soak up the aftermath

The best part about drinking and driving is the creative ways in which you can approach the aftermath. A hilton doesn't just surrender the limelight. Instead, she arranges immediately to be photographed going to church and then playing with the cutest dog ever. Two bitches—every man's fantasy. Smart, Mischa!

PUT THE "HO" IN HOLLYWOOD

Sex in Hollywood isn't a new thing, and it's not so different now than it was fifty years ago. Did you know that in the late 1950s, Jayne Mansfield carefully staged exposing her breasts in several public "accidents"? Apparently, the press responded with editorials that said things like, "We get

Dear Lindsay,

I don't pretend to understand your generation in Hollywood, but of the bunch, you strike me as the only one worth a damn. Cleavage, of course, helped us a lot to get where we are. I don't know how Paris, Nicole, Mischa, Keira, or that girl . . . what's her name . . . Vanessa Hudgens got there. You've been good about giving the twins fresh air, but less good about keeping a lid on the box. In my day, girls like Marilyn and I did Playboy. It's a classy publication, and you can quip something sharp when they ask you what you wear to bed or what you had on during the photo shoot: Chanel No. 5 and the radio, for example. But instead you have pictures on the Internet of your mustard pot looking like it insulted Joe Louis's mother, and when they ask why you posed nude for New York magazine, you say, "I didn't have to put much thought into it." Darling, you make us "dumb blondes" of the past sound positively like George Bernard Shaw. But unlike most of your fellow hiltons, you are an actress—you have some talent, and you can get someone clever to write your lines. If you can remember that and act accordingly, when they say, "Here they are, Lindsay Lohan," they just might be talking about your Golden Globes.

Love and Kisses,
Jayne

P.S. I know everyone scolds you for getting DUIs when you can afford a driver, but trust me, drivers aren't always so great either!

angry when career-seeking women, shady ladies, and certain starlets and actresses . . . use every opportunity to display their anatomy unasked." Nowadays, the press is subtler in its rebukes: "Exclusive! Hot Balcony Sex!" There is no great discrepancy between Britney Spears getting out of a car and flashing her French dip to the whole world and Marilyn Monroe walking over a vent so her white dress blows upward. Except that Marilyn is famous for *covering up.* When I imagine Britney in the same scene, she is struggling to lift up her dress while a strong wind blows it downward.

The hiltons have really been creative and clever when it comes to taking slutdom to a new level, and you've got to play to win. So put on your finest tank and tight jeans, grab your ID, and head out to the hot club of the moment. Don't worry about bringing cash or your credit card—if you're hot and slutty enough, you won't be paying for a thing, except maybe the morning-after pill.

unleash your inner ho-bag

Here are several trusted ways to unleash your inner ho-bag, as learned from the hiltons:

- **SHOW SOME SKIN.** Disney star Vanessa Hudgens went from being a cutesy little crush for straight boys who like musicals (?) to full-blown whack-off material overnight when her nude pictures appeared online. Vanessa's naked-picture scandal is a perfect example of how one photo can catapult you into a whole new category of fame. It's like being the drunk high school freshman girl getting caught blowing the senior quarterback at her first house party—it'll be around the whole school by that eight thirty a.m. class on Monday, and every guy will be obsessed with it. Before the photos, Vanessa was under Zacquisha's shadow, but who's the star now, bitch? Not to be outdone, Ashley Tisdale "accidentally" showed off a little more of her puffy nipple than her Disney execs would have liked while walking the red carpet of an event in July 2007. At least she's twenty-two (even if she plays a teenager in *High School Musical*). On the other hand, Miley Cyrus has already been through several photo scandals by the age of fifteen—suggestive shots with her friends on the Web, photos of her in lingerie and making out with boyfriends, and then, of course, the *Vanity Fair* "nude" photos that got her so much free "bad" publicity.

NIPPLEGATE

During the 2004 Super Bowl halftime show, Justin got a little bit more than he bargained for—and 90 million viewers got a little more than they expected—when he grabbed Janet Jackson's bustier and pulled it off to reveal her nipple (or rather a large, sun-shaped nipple shield). When he did, a new Justin was born. It totally launched him and put him in a whole new light. Remember, he was only recently removed from his boy band days in 'N Sync. For Janet, it made her seem young and sexy again.

● **FLASH THE VAJAYJAY.** A hilton doesn't wear panties, and you shouldn't either. But just because going commando is premeditated and deliberate doesn't mean it's always done with the intention of flashing the cameras. Sometimes you're so high on blow that you forget. Sometimes you leave the house with panties, but you lose them after sex in the club bathroom, and it's confusing. Do you have them on or not? Stop harshing my buzz!

- **SHOP AROUND.** You can never have too many hot dates. Lindsay had a new one every single week, and even hooked up with three guys in a single weekend on the island of Capri. Even in rehab, she is said to have been caught having sex in a toilet stall with a male patient (she's named in his wife's divorce papers). *Us Weekly* had to create flowcharts to keep their readers up to speed. It's possible that in any portion of a recent year, she's slept with over thirty guys. One of LiLo's ex-boyfriends sold a story of her sexual exploits: how she loved to have four orgasms in one sitting and go at it all night long. Go, Lindsay! She could turn me straight! No matter what town or even what country she's in, Linds is never without a man (or a SaMANtha). LezLo's got hos in different area codes! Lindsay goes after what she wants. She is a vicious predator when it comes to the sex hunt. She will eye a guy from across the room and let it be known that right then and there she wants to hit it. One lover, Alessandro Di Nunzio, an *Italian* in a *rock band,* said, "She just kept staring at me. It was unnerving." This was in a country that in 2001 ruled that grabbing someone's ass is not sexual harassment, as long as the act was not premeditated!

- **START EARLY.** It's never too early to start eating pillow like a hilton! Drew Barrymore was getting hammered by Hollywood's elite at the age of, like, what, ten? Now, that's ambition! She was roller-skating to the hottest parties and doing Jell-O shots and blow before she was even old enough to get her learner's permit.

- **FUEL RUMORS.** There's nothing you can do to fuel rumors better than hard-core drinking and partying like *The Hills* star Lauren Conrad. And, of course, have a rumored sex tape that ultimately gets you nicknamed "Beef Curtains" because of your giant vaginal lips! Oh, could there be a more horrifying rumor than that? Yet, she loves the attention. If she didn't, she'd go into hiding and would never be seen out partying. Kudos to her!

- **IF YOU MAKE A SEX VIDEO, YOU NEED TO MAKE IT GOOD!** You'll also need to handle the publicity and marketing of the video as well as any hilton. You need to know what you are going to gain from your video. Paris got millions of dollars, a ratings boost for her show's debut, and the covers of magazines. Then, just when the PR was dying down, she was spotted "shoplifting" the video from a local newsstand. That got the PR machine going again. Later, just weeks before she was to find out that 97 percent of her inheritance would go to charity, she was spotted again in a store wreaking havoc

Rick Salomon is now the most sought-after fuck in Hollywood! Just tape yourself going to town on Paris Hilton, and the next thing you know, you'll be banging Lindsay Lohan and Pam Anderson!

NOTE TO GUYS

over the video, to give it a little more press, and therefore a little more money in her pocket. To this day, it's probably the best-marketed, best-selling, best-publicized sex tape in history. Pam and Tommy may have been the first, but Paris set a new standard. So anticipate the publicity and marketing challenges ahead of you; then leak it!

HOW TO LEAK YOUR SEX TAPE

1. Send it to me; I'll put that skank video up on my site.
2. "Oops, it got stolen from my house!"
3. Get a middleman to distribute it for you. Paris's was given to Red Light District Video—they do good work.
4. Put it on the Web. "How ever did those photos get out there? I'm *soooo* ashamed!"

After Pam and Tommy was Paris; then Kim Kardashian made a sex tape of herself getting nailed by Ray J. Then all of Hollywood seemed to have sex tapes! Fred Durst, Rob Lowe, Kid Rock, Bret Michaels, Vince Neil, Tom Sizemore, Tonya Harding, Colin Farrell, even Dustin Diamond, aka Screech from *Saved by the Bell!* Unfortunately he wasn't going to town on A. C. Slater—how funny would that have been? Mr. Belding could have joined in with some handcuffs and lube!

PEREZ GOSSIP

When Kim started getting too much press from her sex video, Paris dumped her as a friend! Hmm . . . was the timing a coincidence?

give head to get ahead

On any given day, the number one Googled names on the Internet are Britney Spears, Lindsay Lohan, and Paris Hilton, three girls whose vajayjays can be seen by anyone who knows how to turn off SafeSearch.

There's no dillydallying in Hollywood. First base? Second base? In Hollywood there's nothing but home runs, by the way! No dude in Hollywood is going to stick around with the likes of a Paris Hilton or a Lindsay Lohan if they are going to stop them at first base. If guys in Hollywood just wanted first base, they'd be cuddling with Anne Hathaway.

It's well-known within the Hollywood community that E! talk show host Chelsea Handler had a show, it bombed, and then she got another show. How'd it happen? Well, she was fucking the head of the network. He was married to another woman. Now he's dating Chelsea. Bingo!

Bet you're wondering how I got *my* show. I'll never tell! Ahhahaa!

wreck a home

If you steal a mate, do it right! Angelina Jolie appears to be a real-life home wrecker. She's a total beyotch who has a thing for married men, and I still love her. We all still love her. We probably love her more now than before, even though she and Brad were allegedly having an affair during the filming of *Mr. and*

Mrs. Smith. She pulled it off in true hilton style. On the other hand, Claire Danes wrecked both a home and her reputation. She started going out with Billy Crudup while he was with Mary-Louise Parker, who was seven months pregnant, and I instantly started hating her. Claire got hers—they broke up soon after, and what has happened to her life and career since?

Obviously, it helped in Angelina's case that Jennifer Maniston wasn't pregnant. It also helped that Angelina had recently adopted a child from a third-world country. So if you're going to steal someone's man, you'd better be the hottest woman on the planet, and you'd better save the world and all its children while you're doing it.

No dude in Hollywood is going to stick around with the likes of a Paris Hilton or a Lindsay Lohan if they are going to stop them at first base.

After fourteen years of marriage, Shania Twain and Robert "Mutt" Lange split amid rumors of his infidelity with Marie-Anne Thiébaud, thirty-seven, a longtime secretary and house manager at their Switzerland estate. I'm all for cheating with someone superhot, but why cheat with someone like Marie, who is average, ugly, and plain? Especially when your wife is Shania! I mean, have you *seen* the husband? The man is called Mutt for a reason. He lucked out, and then he wasted it all on the help.

Britney Spears snatched Kevin Federline from a pregnant Shar Jackson and married him in September 2004. Jackson says the truth came out only after he flew abroad for a commercial—which became an extended trip with Spears. For some reason, Shar doesn't get the sympathy I would expect. People should like her more; it's not her fault she got screwed over by Britney. But you know what? Look what happened to both Britney and K-Fed since then. Karma can be a real bitch!

Julia Roberts snatched Danny Moder from his wife, and she married him just two months after he got the divorce! Of course, she got her little twins out of the whole deal, so you can't hate her too much. I don't know what Danny's ex-wife looks like, but how can you compete with Julia Roberts? Julia sweearrrss Danny's marriage to his ex was already over when she got involved with him. Okay, well, that settles it!

Tori Spelling and Dean McDermott were married Sunday, May 7, 2006, on a private tropical island in Fiji. They met in Ottawa while filming the TV movie *Mind Over Murder*. Only problem was, at the time, Tori was wed to actor-writer Charlie Shanian, and McDermott was in a twelve-year marriage to Mary Jo Eustace, a Toronto TV personality, and they had a son and an adopted daughter. When he married Tori, Dean said: "I've never had as much of a desire to get married and make a woman my wife as I've had with her. The feeling is overwhelming. We're soul mates." That's Hollywood code for "I'm a desperate star fucker." I don't know why Dean doesn't get more flak for this, but at the same time, I can relate to him. I get it—he was seduced by her fame. She was Tori Spelling, and he was nobody.

In May of 2007, Criss Angel and Cameron Diaz spent a very random few weeks together. Unfortunately, Criss Angel had an estranged "secret" wife, Joanne Sarantakos. Joanne claimed in court that a romance between the Mindfreak and

Cameron occurred during their five-year marriage/fifteen-year relationship. "We're naming Cameron Diaz as his lover," attorney Dominic Barbara said on behalf of Sarantakos. Diaz's rep issued a statement that stated she and Angel first met more than a year after he split from his wife, and went on only four dates, and had no current relationship. This guy is star fucking the whole way. It was smart for his career; he did it again later with Britney Spears. Getting with Cameron Diaz really put this guy on the map. After that, he was able to leverage a $75 million Cirque du Soleil deal at Luxor in Las Vegas.

In February of 2006 (several months *after* the show had taped), *Skating with Celebrities* couple Lloyd Eisler and Kristy Swanson went public with their relationship. The only problem? Lloyd was sort of in a relationship . . . a marriage! He and Kristy went from working together to *sleeping* together. What else do you expect when you spend all day grinding on the cold ice? You need someone to keep you warm. Lloyd and his wife, Marcia, were separated just two weeks before she gave birth to their second child. It's too awful to think about, because Kristy Swanson is not even famous!

Jude Law cheated on fiancée Sienna Miller with his nanny, Daisy Wright. After Law proposed on Christmas 2004, Sienna told reporters, "I'm the happiest girl alive." But in reality, they were off and on after the infidelity, and they split for good in November 2006. The weird thing is, the scandal was the best thing to happen to Sienna. Instead of being Jude Law's girlfriend, she became Jude Law's ex, Sienna Miller, whom he cheated on. It took her up a notch. Next thing you know, she's spotted with Orlando Bloom frolicking around the enchanted wood.

Rose McGowan got with her *Grindhouse* director, Robert Rodriguez. No biggie hooking up with the boss, right? Except that he was married with five kids! Guess Rose did a little more grinding than his wife of sixteen years did!

Hulk Hogan's divorce was occasioned by his hooking up with his daughter's thirty-three-year-old friend Christiane Plante, whom they met while Brooke was recording a song called "They Don't Know About Us." Or *do they*?

have a sexy gay hookup

Hiltons love sex, but after a while, your regular thing gets boring! That's when you need to step onto the field for a same-sex hookup. Whether it's onstage, in a club, in a video, in a movie, or in real life, be sure to make a few plays for the other team— for seconds, nights, or even weeks!

Lindsay's been with practically every guy in Hollywood, so what does she do when she's dog-tired of bone? She chases the cat! Lindsay started dating Samantha Ronson in early 2008 (they had been "friends" forever). Since we couldn't sniff LezLo's fingers, there wasn't much proof that they were dating—until they stepped out in May of 2008, hooking up in Cannes and Paris. Ah, gay Paree!

After splitting up with man-whore Dave Navarro in 2007, Carmen Electra jetted into the sweet embrace of Joan Jett. The two were spotted all over town together, and the rumors began building. I assume Carmen thinks it would kill her career if she actually acknowledged she was gay, since her career equals frat boys beating off to *Baywatch* reruns. Her rep issued a statement saying they were "just friends." Right. Friends with benefits! Of course, Carmen would rather you *not* know which team she plays for—she gets better publicity and more conversation out of it that way!

Remember Britney and Madonna's 2003 VMA onstage kiss? I thought that would cure Britney of any same-sex curiosity forever, like those religious summer camps people were sent to in the 1950s. I guess it wore off, because more than four years later, she was reportedly caught up in a lesbian romp in an LA hotel pool. She's just country, y'all!

Angelina Jolie's lesbian ex-lover Jenny Shimizu (they met in 1996 and dated off and on for several years) seems to be fingering and telling: "She loves women too much. It's like a drug and she was hooked." Angelina admits her lesbian past, but says, "I've never hidden my bisexuality, but since I've been with Brad, there's no longer a place for that or S and M in my life." Well, there is one place: on film—she played a lesbian in *Gia and* appeared in an artsy short film where she "plays" a completely naked model getting it on with another chick, separated by only a chain-link fence.

be sure to make a few plays for the other team—

I don't believe either one of these gals is gay, but that didn't stop Paris Hilton and Elisha Cuthbert from locking lips in January of 2008 at NYC hotspot Tenjune. Just prior to that kiss, Paris had attended the launch party for a new season of *The L Word* and had also visited Los Angeles gay hot spot the Falcon Club. With all that going on around her, the suggestible girl probably just forgot for a few minutes that she wasn't gay.

Whether it's Madonna in real life (with former "girlfriend" lesbians Ingrid Casares and Sandra Bernhard) or Jen Aniston and Courteney Cox hooking up on a season finale of *Dirt* (it didn't save the show), all hiltons go gay for a minute. Tila Tequila even used her supposed bisexuality to get her reality show talked about; the *New York Post*'s Page Six claimed she's not really gay and that she used bisexuality as a publicity stunt and she's actually straight! It's the fad of the moment for heteros. In the nineties everyone was trying to be black, and now they are trying to be gay!

perez hilton's greatest sluts of all time

Lindsay Lohan! Aaron Carter, Wilmer Val-diarrhea, Colin Farrell, Damien Fahey, Talan Torriero, David Spade, Jared Leto, Sean Lennon, Ryan Adams, Brett Ratner, Brody Jenner, Joe Francis, Jamie Burke, Brandon Davis, Harry Morton, Robbie Williams, Jude Law, James Blunt, Calum Best, Criss Angel, Riley Giles, Adrian Grenier, Stavros Niarchos, Samantha Ronson—she's been linked to half of Hollywood! That's not even counting the rumors, which would add Bruce Willis, Leonardo DiCaprio, Shia LeBeouf, Ryan Phillippe, Shawn White. . . .

Paris Hilton! She had a sex tape and goes through men like underpants. Wait, bad simile.

Anna Nicole Smith! She was hooking up with her lawyer, her five-hundred-year-old husband, her friend

Larry, her Bahamian immigration minister, a few ladies, and anyone else who was game.

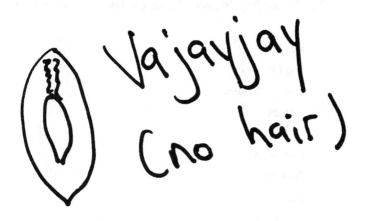

Marilyn Monroe! Flashing of her skirt, singing a sexy "Happy Birthday" to the fucking president of the United States, banging Joe DiMaggio, and taking nude photos even in the sixties. She's one of Hollywood's first true sluts!

Sharon Stone! Here's how Sharon Stone got famous: by flashing her cooch. So how did this serious actress follow it up? By flashing her cooch again in *Basic Instinct 2*!

Britney Spears! She is rumored to have cheated on Justin with Wade Robson, banged Fred Durst, Criss Angel, and Colin Farrell, married a guy for fifty-five hours because she was on Ecstasy (or so says Jason Alexander, the guy she married, who then sold her out!), stolen her backup dancer Kevin from his pregnant baby mama, Shar Jackson, hooked up in the bushes with a guy she met in rehab, and then dated a paparazzo!

Karrine "Supahead" Steffans! The author of *Confessions of a Video Vixen* makes Lindsay look like she's still in *Parent Trap*. Supahead claims to have had sex with:

50 Cent

Big Punisher

Busta Rhymes

Canibus

Clipse

Common

Da Brat

DMX

Fabolous

Fat Joe

Ghostface Killah

Ja Rule

Jay-Z

Kanye West

Khujo from Goodie Mob

Kool G Rap

KRS-One

Lil Wayne

LL Cool J

Ludacris

M.O.P.

Mase

Master P

Method Man

Missy Elliott

Mobb Deep

Mos Def

Mystikal

Nas

Nelly
Noreaga
Ol' Dirty Bastard
OutKast
Pete Rock
Puff Daddy
Q-Tip
Rakim
Redman
Russell Simmons
Scarface
Snoop Dogg
Talib Kweli
The LOX
Timbaland
Too $hort
Trick Daddy
Twista
Will Smith
Wyclef Jean
Xzibit

SECRET HOOTCH ALERT

Kate Hudson: She pretends she's America's Little Sweetheart, but she's not. She's rumored to have gotten with Justin Timberlake (while he was with Jessica Biel), she's off and on with Chris Robinson (her ex), and is rumored to have been the reason that Owen Wilson tried to kill himself. And let's not forget she was banging Dax Shepard forever! Or her "month-mance" with Lance Armstrong.

SECRET HOOTCH ALERT

Nicole Kidman: Tom Cruise, Steve Bing, Q-Tip, Lenny Kravitz, and Keith Urban, and that's just what we know of.

Mrs. Cruise

HOOK UP, NOT DOWN

It's not enough to make wise, self-destructive, fame-affirming changes as you climb toward your goal of becoming a hilton—you also need to make sure you don't take any long slides backward. One thing you certainly *cannot* do is date someone for the wrong reasons, and that's any reason other than raising your celebrity status. The last thing you need is to get to the point where you are fabulous and hot and then blow it by banging some record producer or cosmetic dentist. Or even worse, marrying one! Then the only thing anyone will ever say about you or your husband is, "Huh?"

the ellen pompeo syndrome

Sometimes a star is weak and can't take the pressure of the scene, not unlike a sick wildebeest on *Nature*. She finds some regular person to "ground" her. And I don't mean like a wire; I mean like a plane. She dates or marries outside of her fabulous elite circle, totally blowing her shot at superstardom. Bitches, don't let that be you! I slept through all of my math classes, too, so let's keep it need-to-know:

$$1 + 1 = 2$$

but

$$1 + 0 = 0$$

Yes, it actually equals zero. If you date or marry a nobody, then you become a nobody, and no one will care about you. Consider yourself forgotten, and don't count on being seen or getting on *Access Hollywood* ever again. Your fame is over.

Need an example? Matt Damon married Luciana Barrosa. Who? My point exactly. She wasn't on any celebrity radar, and Matt loved that. She's a former waitress with a child of her own from a previous relationship. Did you tune out before the end of that last sentence? Because I did. Now Matt is totally boring. He obviously wanted out of the Hollywood scene. Wish granted! He's a nobody now. What's that? He was *People* magazine's 2007 "Sexiest Man Alive"? More like *People* magazine's "Sexiest Man Alive Whom We Haven't Already Featured on Our Cover," since they had already awarded the honor to George Clooney, Mateo McConaughey, Dad Pitt, and even McDreamy. They just ran out of actors to feature.

> **One thing you certainly cannot do is date someone for the wrong reasons, and that's any reason other than raising your celebrity status.**

I like to call this phenomenon "the Ellen Pompeo Syndrome." Ellen Pompeo is on *Grey's Anatomy,* the hottest show of the last decade, but no one cares about her. Why? Because she married a "normal." If she were even just *dating* a celebrity, she'd be more famous. Being famous may not be her goal, but ultimately her marriage is the reason she's not a bigger star. She went from being the star of the show to playing second fiddle to Katherine Heigl.

Katherine Heigl married Josh Kelley. He's a D-lister, but he's a musician, and he is at least trying to make a name for himself. If Ellen Pompeo had dated even him, she would have gone up a notch.

Think about it this way: If you're going to a dinner party and you bring a date who is far inferior to you and your friends in all categories—not as hot, not as smart, and not as fabulous—no one will want to talk to you. They'll be polite, but no one will ask what you're doing later or offer to fetch your drinks. Superficial? Totally! But imagine you bring some smokin'-hot superdate who—*oh, by the way*—happens to be *a famous celebrity?* Bam! You're the belle of the ball, and your douche bag friend who brought an accountant is the new Ellen Pompeo, standing in the corner and seething with jealousy.

date up the right way

Look at Kim Kardashian. No one knew who this girl was until she was spotted going to the movies *once* with Nick

Lachey. When the news that she went on a date with Nick first hit the tabloids, Kim was referred to as a "stylist." A stylist! Ha! She went with him to an afternoon showing of *The Da Vinci Code* in West Hollywood, and she completely used that moment to springboard her career. Next thing you know, she's the hottest thing in town! She parlayed a date with Jessica Simpson's ex into bona fide celebrity status. She went from being a stylist to being Nick Lachey's girlfriend to being Paris

Hilton's new best friend (bye-bye, Nicole Richie) to being known as having more junk in the trunk than JLo. She created her own stardom by dating up—that and banging her boyfriend, Ray J, on a sex tape, which for her was the final piece in the puzzle of becoming a hilton. Her fame took on new heights after that. Stardom finally came for her, just like Ray J did! She did all that with one date!

Now, take someone like Justin Timberlake. It would never occur to him to date an ex-waitress or even a backup dancer. Why date someone who is only hot when you can date someone who is hot and also famous? Exactly! Jessica Biel is known for having a killer bod and being gorgeous, but besides a stint on *7th Heaven* and her role in an Adam Sandler movie, um, what else has she done? Justin was clever, because people see Jessica as a notch up because of her looks, even though she is way below Justin in status. He's still the A-lister in the relationship, but he somehow fooled everyone into thinking that he dated up, which he sorta did. That's also why he dated Scarlett Johansson. After breaking up with Britney Spears, who was at the time the hottest thing on the planet, he needed to date Cameron Diaz, who was her equivalent in a different industry. Justin understands that he needs to date someone famous, but she also has to be someone who can "really understand him." It's just like a hilton to use that line, too. Honestly, what's to understand? (And please do see the chart of *selfless geniuses* he recruited to get to the bottom of his complicated psyche.)

If you date or marry a nobody, then you become a nobody . . .

JUSTIN'S DATING CHART:

- Danielle Ditto
- Veronica Finn
- Fergie
- Tatyana Ali
- Britney Spears
- Jenna Dewan
- Janet Jackson
- Christina Aguilera
- Alyssa Milano
- Staci Flood
- Cameron Diaz
- Scarlett Johansson
- Jessica Biel

Lara Flynn Boyle and Jack Nicholson are the ultimate example of dating up. He was sixty-three, she was thirty-three; he was "Jack," she was jack shit! Lara Flynn Boyle was a nobody before she got with him. They dated for a little over a year, from 1999 to 2000, but to this day, it's still what she's known for—being linked to Jack Nicholson. And being scary skinny. And having trout pout. Now she's married to some douche named Donald Ray Thomas II, which gets her *nowhere*. She used to have a career! *Wayne's World, The Temp, Threesome,* then *The Practice.* Since breaking up with Jack, it's been failed TV shows, TV movies, and straight-to-DVD releases.

Who was Catherine Zeta-Jones before she married Michael Douglas? She was in *The Mask of Zorro,* but that was about it. If dating him would send her career skyrocketing, marrying him would send it into another stratosphere! She knew the kind of fame that would come with marrying Michael Douglas. She said, "When Michael told me what was going to happen, I said, 'It's fine.'" Hmmm . . . "It's fine?" It's more than fine, bitch; it is ideal! After she got with Michael, her career did in fact go to another stratosphere: *Entrapment, Traffic, America's Sweethearts,* and an Oscar win for *Chicago.* All that for banging crusty old Michael Douglas! Of course, then there were the T-Mobile commercials—not quite sure why she did that. What's the point of marrying up if you just are going to work down?

Or how about Jerry Seinfeld and Jessica Sklar? In 1998, Jessica had just gotten back from her honeymoon with new hubby Eric Nederlander. Obviously bored in her marriage already (how many days was it? Hahaha!), she started putting the moves on Jerry at the gym. Next thing you know, she's with Jerry and they get married at the end of 1999. She went from being two nobodies, Jessica Sklar and Jessica Nederlander, to being a somebody, Jessica Seinfeld, with one quick stray!

THE ULTIMATE DATING-UP SCENARIO

Ever dream of marrying your idol? Tom Cruise, maybe? Katie always dreamed of marrying Tom Cruise. She had a poster of him up on her wall as a teenager (who didn't?). Now she has his baby! Katie Holmes went from C-list to *superstardom* literally overnight. And she *loves* it. Even though Tom married down, it created "TomKat," and he got even bigger. When he was single, he was a douche and no one cared. Wait, did I say *was* a douche? But now we care!

find a man who dates down

George Clooney has rarely dated anyone famous: Sarah Larson, Krista Allen, Celine Balitran, and Lisa Snowden. Um, who? He likes to be the *man* in the relationship, but he could have been half of the next Brangelina! Bad for him, good for fame whore Sarah Larson. She was a waitress, and she ended up on the cover of *People* magazine! It's not that hard, people—do the right things, play your cards well, and you too could end up dating:

- George Clooney
- Matt Damon
- Jerry Seinfeld
- Denzel Washington
- Patrick Dempsey
- Matthew McConaughey

Not too shabby! Half of Hollywood's starlets would kill to be with those guys, but they're not!

don't divorce up

I wish I could tell you it's as simple as just dating up, but let's look at Ryan Phillippe, who married Reese Witherspoon. You

You've always got to have an exit strategy for when things start getting bad.

can pick a crappy movie to star in, because if it bombs, hey, no big deal; it's out of the theater in a week and forgotten. But if you are stuck in a relationship where your partner gets bigger and bigger while you dwindle, you just look like a loser. And once you break up with them, you'll only end up taking a step down. In 2007, Ryan told *People* magazine, "I signed up for this, and have to deal with it." But I don't think he knew what he was signing. Having hooked up on the set of 1999's *Cruel Intentions,* they were both rising young hot stars in Hollywood. They were destined for stardom together. Unfortunately for him, Reese's career took off without him: *Election, Legally Blonde, Sweet Home Alabama,* and of course, *Walk the Line,* for which she won an Oscar for Best Actress (aka dagger to Ryan's heart). On the other side of the bed, Ryan's career had stalled after they got together. Ryan's films (*Antitrust, The Way of the Gun*) were tanking, while Reese was raking in $20 million paydays, and he was living in her shadow. He married laterally, but he divorced up! Then, as things went sour with her, it was like all of a sudden he got his mojo back. They divorced in 2007 (after over eight years of marriage), and his biggest role ever, *Breach,* came right on the heels of his divorce! Go figure.

Why date someone who is only hot when you can date someone who is hot and also famous?

You've always got to have an exit strategy for when things start getting bad. If I were Ryan and I saw the marriage going south, I would go out and cheat. Because I made the first move, it wouldn't look like I just got dumped. Oh, wait—reportedly, he did that. Smart!

be a supercouple

By merging the two hottest commodities on the planet, Brad and Angelina upped their stock in celebrity. Remember when Angelina was just a single mom who had recently divorced Billy Bob Thornton? She wasn't at goddess status until she got with Brad. Angelina gives all the wild girls hope. All of the slutty drug addicts can one day marry Brad Pitt and have his children. Maybe in five years, Paris Hilton will be the next Angelina Jolie. That would be the ultimate transformation. She'd have, like, five kids and create the Paris Hilton Foundation: "Making the world a hotter place."

GET A NICKNAME!

TomKat, Vaughniston, Minnillo-Blah-Nick, Bennifer—you need a cool handle. Who wants to be half of Brad and Jen when you can be half of *Brangelina*?

There are very few supercouples out there: Brad and Angelina, David Beckham and Victoria Beckham, Heidi Klum and Seal, Will Smith and Jada Pinkett, Jay-Z and Beyoncé, Tom Cruise and Katie Holmes. They are the couples who make everyone think, *Wow, they must have amazing sex.*

WHAT HILTONS ARE THINKING WHEN THEY ARE DOING THE NASTY

You know celebrities must have thoughts in their heads when they are having sex. I'm sure that while Will Smith is banging Jada, he's at some point thinking something like, *I'm Will Smith! I'm banging Jada Pinkett! I'm Will Smith banging Jada Pinkett right now!* How can he not? I'm also pretty sure Jessica Simpson does this, but not during sex, more like, *I'm brushing my teeth right now!* What else could she be thinking about? Here are some other peeks into the minds of celebrities in flagrante delicto:

Keira Knightley: *I wish I could swallow, but the calories . . .*

Victoria Beckham: *Gentle! Hollow bones!*

Heidi Klum: *The clap gets you no fish!*

Jason Wahler: *Are the curtains closed?*

Amy Winehouse: *I hope I was born with that hole.*

Tom Cruise: *When Tom Cruise sees his wife naked, he has to stop, because he knows he's the only one who can help.*

Woody Allen: *Who's your daddy? Oh, God, that's just wrong—I should call my therapist. I'll just think of something wholesome, like how old Scarlett Johansson was when she lost her virginity. No . . . I should definitely call my therapist.*

REPLACE A SNACK WITH CRACK

Hollywood's got an addictive personality, and drugs are addictive. It's *not* a good match, unless you're a drug dealer. Then it's perfect!

Everyone in Hollywood does coke. I would say blow in Hollywood is like alcohol at a high school house party: It's technically illegal, but it's the reason everyone showed up to the event, and everyone is doing it. If you don't, you are branded a loser, and no one will want to hang out with you. And if you do it and get caught, then you're a druggie! See, it is just like high school!

Here's the difference between drugs in Hollywood and drugs in America: Drugs in America are dealt in back alleys, street corners, and run-down apartment buildings. Drugs in America are violent, dirty, and come with serious baggage. But in Hollywood? Rodeo Drive instead of back alleys. Hollywood Hills instead of street corners. Mansions instead of run-down apartment buildings. They get delivered in Ferraris and Hummers. They don't come with baggage; they come in Louis Vuitton luggage.

Smoking weed in Hollywood is like drinking water in other places—it's something you do with your parents at the dinner table. Snorting coke is like smoking a cigarette, because you sneak off to do it, and you feel a bit like a badass. But smoking an actual cigarette in Hollywood is like murdering a puppy who is also an orphan.

ARE YOU COOL, MAN?

In 1999, someone called the fuzz with a noise complaint at two thirty a.m. What did the cops find? They smelled marijuana and found some stems, seeds, paraphernalia, and a nekked Matthew McConaughey playing the bongos. You just gotta keep on livin', man. L-I-V-I-N'.

A hilton runs the risk of getting caught as much as the average person, but at worst she has to go to some fancy rehab. She just makes a public apology; then she walks away with a slap on the wrist. Only the ugly and poor go to jail.

DRUG MEMORY LANE

This might ruin *The Wizard of Oz* for you, but our lovely little Dorothy was quite the druggie. You bitches won't remember this, because she died of an overdose before you were born, but Judy Garland was the Lindsay of her times. It's always been and always will be: *"There's no business like show business, like snow business, like blow."*

A hilton wants to stay up *all damn night.* Most normal people get tired after a certain time. I get tired at ten p.m.! Look, if someone is up until five a.m. three nights in a row, you know they are getting a little help. Britney's infamous bender in the seventy-two hours leading up to her forced hospitalization? She *definitely* had a little help staying up. It wouldn't be the first time, according to Britney's former body-guard of two months, Tony Barretto, who told the media

If you can't do your drugs in the car before you head into the club, and you don't have a bodyguard with a blanket, make sure you go to the *right* kind of club to do them. For instance, the VIP section in NYC's the Box has curtains you can pull around the table for privacy, no bodyguard required!

PEREZ NOTE

he saw Britney doing drugs on at least two occasions in a nightclub. The best part? He says, "She had me hold up a curtain, to make her area private." Yeah, how suspicious does that look?

follow the drug rules:

- **KEEP IT PRIVATE.** Making five or six trips to the bathroom in a one-hour period at a hot club is *not* keeping things private. We know what you're doing! The more drugs you do, the more privacy you're going to need. Why do you think the Olsen Twins are so sneaky and protected? I'm not saying they do drugs—but, uh, what the hell are they hiding then?

- **BE SMART ABOUT WHO YOU DO DRUGS WITH!** Remember that Heath Ledger video that surfaced in the days following his death? It was basically him hanging out at a drug party in LA's Chateau Marmont while his wife and daughter slept in another part of the hotel. This is an era of cell phone cameras and minicamcorders. Even when you don't think anyone is watching, they are watching. It's not 1984 anymore!

- **MAKE SURE THAT YOU HAVE ENOUGH MONEY AND FAME TO BUY YOU OUT OF ANY JAIL TIME.** In the world of celebrity, there are no consequences. For the longest time, Britney thought she could do whatever she wanted and not be held accountable, unlike the little people who get fired from their jobs, sent to jail, lose their kids, or die. But those realities rarely exist for a hilton. They live in the Hollywood bubble and think life is very forgiving, and it is, until it isn't.

GOING TO REHAB FOR DRUG OR ALCOHOL ABUSE IS A TIME-HONORED HILTON TRADITION

- **DEAL WITH THE HANGOVER IN STYLE!** You know that feeling after a hard night of partying that you get the next morning? Massive headache, can't move your body, need about a gallon of water, seven Tylenols, a cheesesteak sandwich, four tubes of Aveeno, a massage, and ten more hours of sleep? Yeah—*that* feeling. Hiltons get that feeling, but they also get all of the aforementioned treatments with a snap of the fingers, bitches! They can pAArty hAArd till the sun comes up but *never* be seen looking like an addict, a zombie, or a cokehead. You just don't see it. They don't have to drive to their corporate veal pen the next morning and remember to use the new cover sheets on their TPS reports. They have remedies brought to their suites by bellhops in cute hats.

- **"JUST SAY NO" PUBLICLY.** Paris Hilton denied doing drugs in her Larry King interview, but there are pictures and videos of her doing various drug activities. Unlike so many of the party girls in young Hollywood, she's never been to rehab, and somehow she manages to stay out till four a.m. and then be up at eight a.m. There's a reason the hiltons are named after her!

CAN I CHARGE IT TO THE ROOM?

Remember Britney's first marriage in Vegas; you know the one—it lasted less than three days? Allegedly, she got married because she was totally rolling on Ecstasy. Someone got it for her because she asked . . . when you become a hilton, no one will ever say no to you.

go to rehab

Going to rehab for drug or alcohol abuse is a time-honored hilton tradition, even though Paris herself has never done it. She has also never been booked for possession, which is something we can't say about many of her imitators. She is the original and the master, so don't feel bad—you've still got some pretty impressive company in rehab, and plentiful, too:

A. Whitney Brown	Chris Penn
Al Unser Jr.	Chris Webber
Alice Cooper	Christian Slater
Amy Winehouse	Christopher Kennedy
Andy Dick	Lawford
Anna Nicole Smith	Chyna
Annie Leibowitz	Colin Farrell
Bela Lugosi	Corey Feldman
Ben Affleck	Corey Haim
Betty Ford	Courtney Love
Billy Bob Thornton	Daniel Baldwin
Billie Holiday	Danny Bonaduce
Bo Bice	Darryl Strawberry
Bobby Brown	David Bowie
Boy George	David Crosby
Brett Butler	David Gahan
Britney Spears	David Hasselhoff
Buzz Aldrin	David Soul
Carrie Fisher	Demi Moore
Charlie Sheen	Dennis Quaid
Chevy Chase	Diana Ross
Chris Farley	Dick Cheney

Dick Van Dyke

Dionne Warwick

Dock Ellis

Dr. John

Drew Barrymore

Dwight Gooden

Eddie Money

Eddie Van Halen

Eileen Brennan

Elizabeth Taylor

Elton John

Eminem

Etta James

Eva Mendes

Fergie

Franz Wright

George C. Scott

George Carlin

George Jones

Gerry Cooney

Glen Campbell

Grace Slick

Haley Joel Osment

Hank Williams III

Iggy Pop

Isaiah Washington

J. Paul Getty Jr.

James Brown

James Frey

James Gandolfini

Jan-Michael Vincent

Jason Priestley

Jason Wahler

Jean-Claude Van
Damme

Jenna Bush

Jennifer Capriati

Jerry Garcia

Jesse Metcalfe

Jessica Hahn

Jessica Sierra

Jim Brown

Jim Ramstad

Jo Dee Messina

Joaquin Phoenix

Joe Louis

Joe Namath

John Belushi

John Daly

John McVie

Johnny Cash

Johnny Depp

Jonathan Rhys Meyers

Judy Carne

Judy Collins

Justin Chambers

Kate Moss

Keith Moon

Keith Richards

Keith Urban

Kelly Osbourne

Ken Caminiti

Kiefer Sutherland

Kirsten Dunst

Kirstie Alley

Kurt Cobain

Larry Hagman

Lawrence Taylor

Leif Garrett

Lenny Bruce

Leonard Nimoy

Lindsay Lohan

Liza Minnelli

Mackenzie Phillips

Marion Barry

Mark Foley

Martin Lawrence

Mary Tyler Moore

Matthew Perry

Mel Gibson

Melanie Griffith

Michael Douglas

Michael Jackson

Mickey Rourke

Mike Tyson

Naomi Campbell

Nell Carter

Nick Carter

Nick Nolte

Nicole Richie

Noelle Bush

O. J. Simpson

Oliver Stone

Onterrio Smith

Ozzy Osbourne

Pat Day

Pat O'Brien

Patrick Kennedy

Patrick Swayze

Paul Williams

Paula Poundstone

Pete Doherty

Philip Seymour Hoffman

Prince Harry

Randy Moss

Ray Charles

Ray Kroc

Richard Carpenter

Richard Dreyfuss

Richard Lewis

Richard Pryor

Richie Sambora

Rick James

Robbie Williams

Robert Blake

Robert Downey Jr.

Robert F. Kennedy Jr.

Robert Mitchum

Robin Williams

Rodney King

Roy Simmons

Rush Limbaugh

Samuel L. Jackson

Scott Weiland

Shelley Winters

Steve Howe

Stevie Ray Vaughan

Tara Conner

Tatum O'Neal	Tonya Harding
Ted Kennedy	Truman Capote
Ted Turner	Vitas Gerulaitis
Tim Allen	Whitney Houston
Tom Arnold	Wilson Pickett
Tom Sizemore	Winona Ryder
Tony Curtis	Wynonna Judd

And that's just off the top of my head.

Jack Nicholson has always been rumored to like the white powder. Even at his age, he allegedly requested a special sex scene in *The Departed* where his female partner's tush would appear to be dusted with coke!

PEREZ TIP

model yourself after one of the greats

It's difficult for many young people to find a role model these days. Baseball players use steroids, Disney stars can be seen nude on the Internet, competitive cyclists are blood doping, the president and vice president have DUIs, and Kelly Clarkson can't produce a hit single to save her life. The one area where there is no shortage of inspirational role models is when it comes to alcohol and substance abuse. So just pick someone from the list above, and use him or her as a blueprint. For example:

Lindsay Lohan

SUMMER 2006—Hospitalized for being "overheated and dehydrated."

NOVEMBER 7, 2006—Tells Oprah she is not a party girl.

NOVEMBER 12, 2006—The *National Enquirer* alleges she overdosed on cocaine and painkillers.

DECEMBER 2006—Tells *People* magazine she has been in AA for a year, and that she feels better when she's not drinking.

JANUARY 17, 2007—Checks herself into the Wonderland Center rehabilitation facility.

MAY 7, 2007—*News of the World* reports that Lindsay was allegedly photographed snorting cocaine with two friends crammed into a bathroom stall at Teddy's nightclub in Hollywood's Roosevelt Hotel.

MAY 9, 2007—The *National Enquirer* reports that she is using massive amounts of cocaine mixed with Ecstasy, taking downers to sleep, and boozing daily.

MAY 26, 2007—Lindsay is arrested and cited for driving under the influence in Los Angeles; police also find cocaine.

MAY 28, 2007—Lindsay checks into Promises in LA.

JULY 13, 2007—Lindsay checks out of Promises in LA.

JULY 13, 2007–JULY 15, 2007—Seen partying at LA hot spot Les Deux and Vegas club Pure.

JULY 20, 2007—Surrenders herself to be fingerprinted and photographed for May 26 arrest.

JULY 24, 2007—Arrested for second DUI in two months. Police find cocaine in pants pocket.

EARLY AUGUST 2007—Checks into Cirque Lodge rehabilitation center. Fails drug test while there.

OCTOBER 5, 2007—Checks out of Cirque Lodge.

NOVEMBER 15, 2007—Reports to the Lynnwood jail to serve her minimum twenty-four-hour sentence as part of her plea deal in her two DUI cases. Gets out eighty-four minutes later.

JANUARY 1, 2008—Captured on video sipping from a champagne bottle at Italy's Capri Film Festival.

JANUARY 25, 2008—Spotted at the Beatrice Inn in New York drinking at least two vodka drinks with professional douche bags Stavros Niarchos and Brody Jenner.

And so on.

BEST HILTON DRUG QUOTES EVER

"They're not mine."

—Lindsay Lohan

★

"It wasn't on me; it was in the car."

—Nicole Richie

★

"My mind seemed to have a huge neon sign in it that blinked nonstop: COKE. GET COKE. So I did."

—Drew Barrymore

★

"Blow would dress you up for a party, but never take you there."

—George Clooney

★

"I ended up on a shrink's couch, and he told me to write down how much I did in a week: 20 Es, 4 grams of coke, 6 of speed, half an ounce of hash, 3 bottles of Jack Daniel's, 12 bottles of red wine, 60 pints."

—Colin Farrell

★

"I would never urinate on the Alamo at nine o'clock in the morning dressed in a woman's evening dress sober."

—Ozzy Osbourne

my solemn promise

I wish I could tell you so much more about drugs in Hollywood. The fact is, since I'm Perez Hilton, not too many people are doing lines in front of me! I mean, the one person a hilton doesn't want to do drugs in front of is me. And you know what? I probably wouldn't do anything in front of me either!

So here's the deal. Just for the sake of it happening, I'll promise now that the next celebrity to do drugs in front of me—my lips are sealed! I swear. The first one gets a free pass. Of course, don't be the second one to do drugs in front of me. Because then you're totally screwed.

$3.99

GET THAT MONEY

Famously, supermodel Linda Evangelista once said, "We don't wake up for less than $10,000 a day." That was 1990, and, my, how times have changed. Can you imagine Gisele Bündchen, who has a personal fortune of $150 million and made $33 million in 2007 alone, doing *anything* for a mere $10,000? That's actually a trick question, because Gisele no longer works for dollars and demands to be paid in euros! How hilton is that?

A hilton demands money to do everything—from making an appearance at a nightclub to giving quotes to a magazine to taking a pee! What are you, a charity organization? No! A magazine wants you for a photo shoot? Make them fly you to Aruba for the shoot and put you up at the Ritz! For five days! With your friends and family! A club wants you to make an appearance? Charge them $10k to walk through the door. Get a VIP table with your friends, free top-shelf bottle service, and a limo to and from. Get paid to get hammered, and do it again the next night!

what you are worth, as a hilton

Pam Anderson gets at least $20,000 to walk into a new club. Las Vegas clubs are the most notorious for this—they'll pay anywhere from $10,000 to $1 million to have a celebrity show up. Lindsay Lohan gets at least $10,000 to go on a shopping spree in your new clothing boutique. Mischa Barton gets $5,000 to dine at a new restaurant. If you are on a reality TV show, you could probably get $2,500 to show up to a club. That's if you're an Olly girl from the show *Sunset Tan* or one of the chosen girls from, like, *Rock of Love* or *Flavor of Love*. Someone like Brody Jenner can make $5,000 a night. If you are *The Hills* star Lauren Conrad, you can make $10,000. If you are *the* Paris Hilton you can make $50,000. She is the queen of selling herself. Realistically, she has an event a week where she gets $50,000 for that event, whatever it may be. She got paid a bunch of money to attend a fashion show in Russia in 2008. For something big like that, she'll get anywhere from $100,000 to $150,000, and that's not including expenses for a hair and makeup team, some friends, a few bodyguards, and anyone else she may need. Get yours!

Of course, New Year's brings the biggest paydays. For 2007's New Year's Eve party, Las Vegas's Pure paid Britney Spears a reported $350,000, and what did she do? The new mom famously fell asleep around one a.m. and had to be helped out of the club. Money well spent! Ashlee Simpson and Pete Wentz reportedly got $150,000 for showing up at the Shore Club in Miami for New Year's 2008. Pam Anderson made $110,000 partying at TAO in Las Vegas in 2007 and switched over to Pure in 2008, probably for even more cash. Paris and Nicky Hilton are rumored to have been paid $500,000 for ringing in the New Year at Las Vegas's LAX.

So who's paying for all of this? Well, not the club alone! A club can't afford it, so they aren't the only ones forking over the cash. Cosponsors help cover the costs. The liquor companies that want a hilton to drink their booze will sponsor the night. The car companies will compete to get a hilton in their limo. The designers compete to get the hilton in their dress. In the end, everything, as always, is taken care of. Getting a hilton into their club or brand is the goal, and no amount of money is too large to make it happen.

> A hilton demands money to do everything—from making an appearance at a nightclub to giving quotes to a magazine to taking a pee! What are you, a charity organization?

Can You Match the Star to the Fee?

1. Jeremy Piven

A) $4 million to sing two songs at Russian billionaire Andrei Melnichenko's wedding

2. *American Idol*'s William Hung

B) $1.2 million to party at Las Vegas club Pure all year

3. Christina Aguilera

C) $4,000 to sing two songs at an event

4. Jennifer Lopez

D) $50,000 to show up at a birthday party for one hour and deliver the dessert tray

5. Paris Hilton

E) $1.2 million to sing for 40 minutes at Russian billionaire Andrei Melnichenko's birthday party

Answer key: 1D, 2C, 3A, 4E, 5B

take what's yours, and that's everything

If you can't get cold, hard cash, there are always gifts. There was even a time when a proper lady accepted *only* these, for some dumb reason!

- Diamonds
- Vacations
- Cars
- Hotel rooms
- Clothes
- Electronics
- Spa treatments
- Plastic surgery
- Shopping sprees

. . . a true hilton will cut a deal with the paparazzi and get paid for the photos, on top of the free clothes!

W2
- jewelry
- Porsche
- free apartment in NYC
- vacations
- bling
- flat screen TV
- shoes
- iPod
- camera
- babies

Companies want a hilton to speed out of *their* hotel parking lot, in *their* swanky convertible, blasting *their* music on *their* stereo system, while wearing *their* tank top and flashing *their* bling. Bentley wants Paris Hilton in their car. The Atelier skyscraper in Manhattan wants LiLo living there. The Chateau Marmont wants Cameron Diaz walking through its lobby. Jacob the Jeweler wants Vanessa Minnillo blinged out in his bling. And you know what? Wish granted!

You'd think the companies win this game, but the person who *really* comes out ahead is the hilton. They can receive upward of a million dollars in gifts per year, if not more. Every day brings a new opportunity to get something new. Let the little people run out to buy things they really can't afford; you will be getting it for free as you sit on your white leather couch counting your millions.

You see pictures of celebrities shopping in stores like Armani Exchange and Intuition. Those places are crawling with hiltons, and it's like the paparazzi are right there inside the stores with them. You know why? Because the paparazzi *are* inside with them! Most of those shopping trips are prearranged, so the hilton walks out of the store with tons of loot—but she didn't pay a thing. That's why everyone *else* has to pay so much! And a true hilton will cut a deal with the paparazzi and get paid for the photos, on top of the free clothes!

If you're not receiving extravagant gifts, it's because you're not hot enough. So a hilton's *got* to work it if she wants to earn money for doing nothing much at all. If you want to be seen with freebies as though you had paid for them, your agent needs to pitch you to various companies, and you need to hit up the clubs, travel the world, and be photographed looking good. A hilton must look hot and rich, regardless of what's really going on. You're not gonna make it driving a Ford Focus to Bennigan's.

take a gift bag

The MTV Video Music Awards, Oscars, Emmys, Sundance, the Grammys, the Golden Globes, the MTV Movie Awards—here comes the free shiz! It seems like every awards show has a special gifting suite. Clothing companies, electronics companies, spas, jewelers, and more set up these rooms where a hilton can just come in and pick out anything she wants. And the best part was, up until 2007, it was all tax-free!

How much do you want to bet that these hiltons forget to mention all their gifts to their accountant ?

But you need to be careful—the gifting suites are crawling with journalists and reporters, and they'll totally rat you out! So pretend you don't *really* want anything, even though you know you desperately want that Guitar Hero bundle. Oh, and the diamond ring. And the sunglasses, and the spa treatment, and the massage session. Pretend you don't care with a "Sure, I'll take it, if they are giving it out." But don't look greedy, and never be seen carrying anything out on your own. Have your assistant pick it up. You don't want the paparazzi getting a shot of you with all of your free loot. Mary-Kate Olsen, Maggie Gyllenhaal, and Leonardo DiCaprio refuse to have their photos taken, but they still grab shit!

SOME PAST OSCAR GIFT-BASKET ITEMS

- A Krups kitchen set ($700)
- Two nights at NYC's Carlyle hotel ($2,300)
- Shu Uemura cosmetics ($600)
- A year of free broadband phone ($500)
- Three nights at South Carolina's Palmetto Bluff ($3,600)
- Two nights at Carmel Valley's Bernardus Lodge ($2,500)
- Three nights at Dana Point's St. Regis Monarch Beach Resort & Spa ($5,900)
- Morton's the Steakhouse dinner ($1,500)
- Cashmere pajamas ($500)
- Assorted olive oils ($540)
- Cornelia Day Resort package ($3,500)
- Three nights at Montecito's San Ysidro Ranch ($3,000)

(Source: *USA Today*)

plug the product

When you walk the red carpet for a big-time event or premiere, make sure you tell them who you are wearing:

Dress by Calvin Klein
Jewels by Neil Lane
Shoes by Jimmy Choo
Glasses by Armani

Ever wonder why a hilton *always* mentions everything she's wearing? Because she didn't pay for any of it! Have you ever heard a hilton say, "I'm not commenting on what I'm wearing. I paid for it, and that's all you need to know"? Never.

Celebrity stylist Rachel Zoe told the *New York Times Magazine* that "if an unknown brand is worn by a certain person in a tabloid, it will be the biggest designer within a *week*." Rachel Zoe is an idiot, but of course she's right.

sell it, don't smell it

After three Paris-inspired perfumes—Paris Hilton, Just Me, and Heiress—Paris's fourth eau de toilette is called Can Can.

Wait, did that joke just write itself? Of course, it could be that the name is a reference to her favorite serving vessel for champagne, since she endorses a *canned* sparkling wine called Rich Prosecco (classy!). She also has a line of hair extensions called DreamCatchers, though whether this refers to the Stephen King horror novel of the same name is a mystery. She's in softcore porn commercials for Carl's Jr. and Hardee's, as well as one for German Yellow Pages. Wait, what? Don't worry; they make it work by having her roll around in a pair of *yellow* panties. Hilton founded Heiress Records on Warner Brothers to put out her self-titled album, *Paris,* and she authored a best-selling book that got better reviews than this one can hope for—the bitch is paid!

Jessica Simpson's got her own line of swimsuits and bikinis, a line of hair extensions, and a line of beauty products, perfumes, shoes, and handbags. She's got everything a woman needs (except a husband). Teri Hatcher was the spokesperson for Clairol. David Beckham got $10 million from Gillette, Beyoncé got almost $5 million from L'Oréal, and Justin Timberlake signed a $6 million deal with McDonald's (yeah, he's pretty much "Lovin' It").

A hilton must look hot and rich, regardless of what's really going on.

The best has to be 50 Cent, though. He invested in and took part ownership of the company that puts out VitaminWater. He made his own grape-flavored water called "Formula 50," which has sold well over 10 million bottles. Fiddy is said to own about 10 percent of VitaminWater and Glacéau, and Coca-Cola recently bought Glacéau for a cool $4.1 billion. That means he made $400 million! Fuck rapping; a real gangsta needs to be in the beverage racket!

I WILL NEVER GO HUNGRY AGAIN

Tara Reid doesn't make money acting anymore; she gets paid to be Tara Reid. She had a big role in *American Pie*, but since then not much has worked in her favor. She's totally milked it to the fullest, though. We're tired of her in the U.S., but she's still valuable overseas. Every year she makes several trips to Australia and the U.K., where bars, clubs, and restaurants will pay her to come hang out. In the end, it just depends on how low you're willing to sink.

walk like an advertisement

Hiltons now even integrate product placement into their lives. Do you think Jennifer Aniston lugs around SmartWater for free? No! She gets a piece of the pie! Paris wears "boyfriend" Benji Madden's DCMA clothing line. Nicky Hilton wears her own Chick line. Stefani has her L.A.M.B, Eve rocks the Fetish, and Ghostface Killah protects his neck with a Wu Wear scarf.

be a designing hilton

Remember when celebrities used to act and make movies and TV shows and sing? Well, most hiltons can't do those things (though some try), so instead they attempt to sell you something other than talent: cotton-spandex blends.

Tara Reid doesn't make money acting anymore; she gets paid to be Tara Reid.

That's right, celebrities who can't even dress themselves without paid stylists are all of a sudden *designing* clothes. Most of them have *no* fashion or design experience, so don't worry if you don't either. It's not like you have to spend countless hours learning about design, colors, materials, and fabrics. It's no different from posing with a big pair of headphones in DJ AM's booth: It doesn't make you a spinner; it's just another way of keeping yourself busy. The only risk is becoming the blue-light special at Kmart.

Nicole Richie has a jewelry line. She is definitely a fashionista, and designing jewelry is a great idea for her. She can make her own line of "jewelry for zombie hands." Madonna and Angelina would both buy it. She's also designing a maternity clothing line—I guess she'll work on it during the downtime on her block-buster movies and TV shows. She says, "It's about showing your best self, not your tired, worn-down self." You know what pregnant women need even more than fashion when they feel tired and worn down? Calories!

Paris Hilton sells T-shirts and designer tops. She also launched a ten-piece jewelry line with Amazon, saying, "This jewelry is for the heiress in everyone." The collection features necklaces, earrings, a charm bracelet, ankle bracelet, and belly chain, and it's priced from $15 to $95. Hundredaires rejoice.

I hate Lauren Conrad's line of clothes—it's so plain and boring and overpriced. If I want plain and boring, let me go to Old Navy, where at least it's cheap. Some of Lauren's dresses cost $185 and look like curtains. On the other end of the spectrum, Heidi Montag's Heidiwood is cheap, just $10 to $60. It looks like hooker wear, but at least if you end up using one of her dresses to clean up after sex, it won't be a complete waste of money.

April 2008, Ashlee Simpson-Wentz premiered a new collection of tops "designed" by her and sold exclusively at Wet Seal. Soon after, Wet Seal realized how shitteous the line was doing and started practically giving it away for free! The collection started out marked at $19.50, but after a month they were sold on Wet Seal's Web site for just $4.99, cheaper than a latte! Poor Asslee. I'd still recommend buying one of her T-shirts over one of her albums, though!

Nicky Hilton has Chick by Nicky Hilton and also Nicholai (her real name is Nicholai Hilton). It all sucks, because she's not a real designer. Seriously, have you ever asked someone, "Where did you get that top?" and they responded with, "Oh, it's Nicholai by Nicky Hilton"? No. Never happens. I've never known *anyone* who wears it. The only person who wears Nicky Hilton is her boyfriend when she's all over him.

The Olsen Twins have the Row and Elizabeth and James. Their style has gotten better over the years, which is a good thing, because they used to dress like they were homeless. Now

Hiltons have figured out a way to make everything they do an opportunity to make money.

they make "slouchy cardigans, shrunken blazers, a leopard-print coat." The Row is sold in Barneys New York, but have you ever heard of anyone wearing it? I haven't. They design both lines themselves, even doing their own sketches. (Isn't it funny that they need to state that?) Of course, don't forget the Mary-Kate and Ashley line, for ages five to twelve, at Wal-Mart. That one actually sells.

Because she is neither a designer nor a nurse, Katherine Heigl has designed her own line of scrubs. Lindsay Lohan is launching a line of her favorite apparel, leggings (with knee pads). So basically, just think of the stupidest thing you can, designed by the least-qualified person in the world, and then sell it to the people who saw *Caffeine* and *I Know Who Killed Me*.

Even I'm pimping my shiz at Hot Topic! What are you waiting for?

sell your photos

Hiltons have figured out a way to make everything they do an opportunity to make money. They open up their homes to a magazine for an "at home" photo shoot. *Cha-ching!* They call the paparazzi to photograph them shopping. *Cha-ching!* They invite the paparazzi to watch them swim on the beach, walk their dog, go to church, exercise, get speeding tickets, take a dump—whatever!

The fastest way to make money *and* control your image is to set up your own paparazzi shoot. When Mischa Barton was trying to fix her image after getting pulled over for a DUI, she set up *two* photo shoots, and Mischa was getting a cut of the photo sales from the paparazzi—tens of thousands of dollars at least. It's not like Mischa is raking in millions from her big-time movie and TV roles. In fact, she doesn't have any major roles! Her role is being Mischa. *The Hills* stars Spencer Pratt and Heidi Montag do it several times a week, and their photos get syndicated all over the world. There's a ton of money to be made—Eva Longoria took in $2 million for exclusive photos of her wedding, as did Mariah Carey. Demi and Ashton's wedding photos netted them $3 million from *OK!* magazine. A mere $1 million got *People* magazine the exclusive photo rights to Ashlee Simpson's wedding to Pete Wentz. Only the little people spend money to have a wedding; a hilton actually turns an obscene profit! It's the same with having a baby.

> **The fastest way to make money *and* control your image is to set up your own paparazzi shoot.**

WHAT IT COSTS TO BE A HILTON

It's not like exploiting yourself and everyone else for money needs justification, but if it did, consider this: Being filthy rich can buy you a lot of things, including amazingly ridiculous material goods and even fame itself, but at some point it takes *zillions* to maintain it, instead of just millions. Millions dry up real fast between cars, homes, food, clothes, jewelry, travel, luxury goods, spas, upkeep, plastic surgery. It's impossible to gauge what a Hilton actually spends to maintain the good life, but just the basics add up to more than what the average "celebrity" actually earns. Believe it or not, *very few* celebrities actually charter their own private jets when traveling. You've got to be severely A-list and loaded in order to make that happen. We know the Jen Anistons, Brad and Angelinas, and Demi and Ashtons do it, but if you're just Hilary Duff or Usher or Nicole Richie, Megan Fox, Shia LeBeouf, or even Teri Hatcher, you're sitting on the Delta tarmac . . . *just like us!* Okay, they may be in first class—but it ain't private, is it?

So if you want to just buy your way into the lifestyle of a hilton, and not go the route of being anorexic, getting arrested, and courting death—that is, actually *being* a hilton—here's what your tab is going to look like at the end of the day:

CAR: $175,000

First, you've got to drive the right kind of car. As we know, you're never going to get into the hottest clubs if you show up in a Ford Escort. Maybe a Toyota Prius for the whole Hollywood-faux-green angle, but really, it's got to be something flashy. You should roll like Paris does—she's been cruising around for a few years in her $175,000 Bentley. And you've got to treat your $175,000 Bentley like it's a piece of shit. Paris has been involved in just as many fender-benders and traffic violations in her Bentley as someone with a hoopty-mobile would have. Even her ex-boyfriend Stavros Niarchos scratched it up. She's gotten tickets in it, had it towed, and even once reportedly lost it in a poker bet! Did she pay retail for her Bentley? Probably not! Did she pay for it at all? Probably not! She's given that car way more than $175,000 worth of publicity. So if it was a gift from the company, it was well worth it! But only Paris can get that shit for free. So step one—driving a fancy-schmancy car—that'll put you in the hole $175,000. Of course, that's just one car Paris owns. Jay Leno owns more than fifty cars!

HOME: $1.4 MILLION

Having a luxurious home is just as important as all of the other bullshit in Hollywood. Remember, it's not like the paparazzi stop shooting you when you get home. In fact, since that's where you live, they're more likely to show up there than anywhere else. So you'd better fork out some cash for a place that doesn't make you look poor, and that doesn't come cheap. While the likes of Tom Cruise and Angelina Jolie boast homes from LA to Colorado to New Orleans and places across the world, the rest of Hollywood is forced to duke it out for space in and around the 90210. Take for instance *Ugly Betty*'s America Ferrera. She's not a huge movie star, but she's big enough. It's not like she's raking in the zillions, but she's on a successful TV show. The cost of living where America lives? A mediocre $1.415 million (of course, she got a steal—the house was listed for $2.19 million). If you're a star in LA, that kind of money won't get you very far. It got America a three-bedroom, 3.5-bathroom home with a pool and spa, a gym, and a two-car garage. Cheap by Hollywood standards! Compare it to Brad and Angelina's French château bought in 2008 for $70 million and change. Not bad for an 880-acre estate!

CLOTHES: $150,000

In April of 2008, Fergie dropped $30,000 during a four-hour shopping bonanza at Calvin Klein in NYC. That's $30k in four hours. That's $7,500 an hour. She spent more in an hour on clothes than some people spend in a decade! And she's not alone. You've heard the stories—everyone from Lindsay Lohan to Jennifer Lopez closing down stores so they can have their private shopping sprees. But just imagine, if a hilton can blow $30k in four hours, what do they spend over the course of a year? Typically I'd say the average celebrity (non-A-listers) spends in the range of $100,000 to $200,000 a year on clothes.

FOOD AND DRINK: $500,000

Kevin Federline is a nobody, right? Marrying Britney Spears is all the Federjerk ever did. Well, that and divorcing her. But even Kevin knows how to spend, and he often drops thousands at restaurants. He tips very well, too! He dropped a $1,100 tip on a $2,782 bill at an LA restaurant in 2007. The same goes for his strip-club adventures—he once went to Scores and left a $2,000 tip on a $365 bill. Some of his other bar bill expenditures? $3,863 at TAO Nightclub, and $3,008 at the Hard Rock Beach Club. The Federjerk knows how to party!

PLASTIC SURGERY: $100,000

You don't have just one surgery—it's addictive, and it adds up. Demi Moore reportedly gets one practically every day! Her totals vary depending on whom you believe. Some say millions; others say she's had nothing at all (that's laughable). Let's go with the widely publicized cost of over $400,000. While Demi's the extreme, Hollywood, of course, loves their little nips and tucks. A few thousand for the nose, a few thousand for each boob—it's not cheap to look pretty!

PRISON: $5,000

Of course, at the end of the day you're not a true hilton unless you spend a little time in the slammer. But even going to jail for a few days isn't cheap . . . for the taxpayers! The average inmate in the Los Angeles County jail system costs taxpayers $99.64 a day, but a hilton's incarceration costs taxpayers

$1,109.78 a day, more than ten times the normal cost! A hilton's tab includes special staff and medical treatment reserved only for the famous. When you're a celebrity, oftentimes the courts make you pay back the money it costs the taxpayers. So in the case of Wesley Snipes and his tax-evasion case? More than $200,000!

FAME: PRICELESS

All of the above? Food, shelter, transportation, clothes, and plastic surgery have already put you in the hole $2 million! But what about first-class travel, five-star exclusive resorts, jewelry, hair and makeup, and all the other expenses the good life costs? Now you see why Mariah has to hawk her wedding photos and Tara Reid agrees to pub appearances in Beerwah. Being famous is expensive!

SELL YOUR FIRSTBORN

There's a new business in Hollywood—baby selling!
And it's not some underground black-market operation, either.
In fact, it couldn't be more public.

In 1989, Lisa Marie Presley's photos of her baby daughter sold for $100,000. Almost twenty years later, *People* magazine kicked out the stops with a staggering $6 million to Jennifer Lopez and Marc Anthony for the first photos of new twins Max and Emme. They also paid a reported $1 million for pictures of Nicole Richie's baby, Harlow; $1.5 million for shots of Christina Aguilera's son, Max; and $500,000 to Britney Spears and Kevin Federline for Sean Preston. *OK!* magazine forked over $575,000 to Gwen Stefani and Gavin Rossdale for baby Kingston's photos, a million for Jamie Lynn Spears's pregnancy story and future baby pictures, and $2 million for Anna Nicole Smith's daughter, Dannielynn. Brad Pitt and Angelina Jolie sold photos of Shiloh for $4.1 million to *People* and got an additional $3.5 million, for the same photos, from UK's *Hello!* magazine (all donated to a mysterious "undisclosed charity"). Brangelina then sold photos of their adopted son Pax to *People* for a reported $2 million. The twins are rumored to have gotten over $12 million!

red carpet suicide

get knocked up right now

Why are you reading this book when you could be getting it on? Having a baby is big business. A real hilton will have a baby just for the money. Think of all of the nannies you could hire for $1.5 million. You'd never even have to take care of the damn kid. Better yet, find yourself a rich baby daddy (or, in Kevin Federline's case, a rich baby mama) and turn seven minutes of heaven into seven decades of payments!

No one does the baby sale better than the baby-selling queen: Tori Spelling. How many times have we seen Tori pregnant, Tori with her kids, Tori the mom, Tori the mom who lost the baby weight? She's in every tabloid out there—she's the master! Does she even *really* work anymore? It's amazing how Tori Spelling has managed to keep herself in the spotlight without working for the last decade. She had a reality show in 2007, but that is about all she's done in the last ten years. Having kids was the best thing she ever did. Tori has had a total rebirth in popularity and has probably made several million dollars off of her babies.

I can see hubby Dean counting between contractions in the delivery room:

"One, one million; two, one million; three, one million; push!"

Who the hell cared about Katie Holmes before Suri? No one! She was on *Dawson's Creek.* Now she's Suri's mom! This could be you! Get yourself a Suri!

IF YOU DON'T HAVE A BABY TO SELL, SNATCH ONE!

- In 1974, actress Julie Andrews and her second husband, Blake Edwards, snatched two orphaned Vietnamese girls, Amy and Joanna.

- Mia Farrow has snatched eleven kids from various countries, including India, Vietnam, and South Korea.

- Madonna swept into Malawi in 2006 to snatch a little boy, David Banda.

- Ewan McGregor and Eve Mavrakis, in April 2006, announced that they had snatched a four-year-old girl from Mongolia.

- Frances McDormand and Joel Coen have a son, Pedro, whom they snatched from Paraguay in 1995.

- Angelina Jolie snatched Maddox Chivan from Cambodia in 2002, Zahara Marley from Ethiopia in 2005, and Pax Thien from an orphanage in Vietnam in 2006.

- Meg Ryan snatched a two-year-old girl from China in 2006.

- Mary-Louise Parker snatched a baby girl from Africa in September 2007.

no moment is too precious to whore out

If you want to be a hilton, you have to be prepared to sell every moment of your life. Go ahead and be shameless about whoring out your baby—but then don't say you hate the paparazzi. Don't say you hate the lack of privacy. If you live in Hollywood and you pimp your kid out to *People* magazine, get ready for him to be a zoo monkey the rest of his life. There will be interest in everything that kid does. First steps, first words, first poopy diaper. Those millions don't come for free. If you want to sell out your kids, you gotta *sell out your kids*.

For Jennifer Lopez, it totally worked, and she came out ahead. Next to Angelina, she became the mother of *People's* highest-selling kids cover ever (around $2 million)! Congratulations, JLo—each of your kids is almost half as interesting as Shiloh ($2.3 million)! But don't think for a second that JLo, Nicole Richie ($1.8 million), and Christina Aguilera ($1.3 million) weren't all crossing their fingers, hoping they'd be number one.

Christina is rumored to have thrown a tantrum and fired her manager, one of her assistants, and her PR firm after getting the disappointing news. Even when you sell out your kids, you're still a mom at heart. It stings!

Go ahead and be shameless about whoring out your baby—

To make sure your kid is the target of as much attention as possible, one easy thing you can do is to saddle him with a regrettable name for life. Here are a few examples of celebrity baby names, which will hopefully give you some inspiration:

1. Arthur Ashe: **Camera**

2. Barbara Hershey / David Carradine: **Free**

3. Bob Geldof : **Fifi Trixibelle**

4. Bruce Willis / Demi Moore: **Tallulah Belle**

5. Christie Brinkley: **Sailor Lee**

6. Erykah Badu / André 3000: **Seven Sirius**

7. Frank Zappa: **Diva Muffin**

8. Gillian Anderson: **Piper Maru**

9. Gwyneth Paltrow / Chris Martin: **Apple**

10. John Cougar Mellencamp: **Spec Wildhorse**

11. Michael Hutchence: **Heavenly Hiraani Tiger Lily**

12. Nicholas Cage: **Kal-el**

13. Penn Jillette: **Moxie CrimeFighter**

14. Robert Rodriguez: **Rebel Antonio**

15. Simon Le Bon: **Saffron Sahara**

16. Sylvester Stallone: **Sage Moonblood**

17. Toni Braxton: **Denim Cole**

Nightmare Mode: Male or female?

Answer key: 1F, 2M, 3F, 4F, 5F, 6M, 7F, 8F, 9F, 10M, 11F, 12M, 13F, 14M, 15F, 16F, 17M

MIX AND MATCH

If creativity isn't your strong suit, use this chart. For each name (usually one to four), roll a die to determine a category, then again to decide a name.

CATEGORY:

1. Spices   2. Occupations   3. Inventions

4. Fruits   5. Qualities   6. Fabrics

Spices:

1. Parsley
2. Marjoram
3. Chervil
4. Tarragon
5. Nutmeg
6. Cilantro

Fruits:

1. Persimmon
2. Tamarind
3. Durian
4. Plantain
5. Guava
6. Pomegranate

Occupations:

1. Sapper
2. Tanner
3. Gumshoe
4. Smithy
5. Hooker
6. Codemonkey

Qualities:

1. Continence
2. Clemency
3. Sovereignty
4. Malice
5. Parsimony
6. Tumescence

Inventions:

1. Satellite
2. Botox
3. Robot Coupe
4. Bidet
5. Router
6. Merkin

Fabrics:

1. Vinyl
2. Spandex
3. Mylar
4. Rayon
5. Velveteen
6. Leather

make your kid your comeback

Got a movie coming out next week? Start showing off your kid! Remember when Katie Holmes had her flop *Mad Money* coming out and she was showing off Suri to all of Manhattan? FAO Schwarz shopping sprees, dinners on the Upper East Side, sidewalk strolls, it didn't matter. Suri was on a tour de Manhattan! And Katie went on *Good Morning America* and every other talk show she could to blab about Suri. You never see Sharon Stone with her kid, except when she's got a movie coming out! It's like she rents the kid on an as-needed basis.

> **If you want to be a hilton, you have to be prepared to sell every moment of your life.**

Getting divorced? Husband an asshole? Take your kids out for a stroll and show them off to the paparazzi! Remember every time Denise Richards and Charlie Sheen got into a bitter war of words what would happen next? Denise would take babies Sam and Lola to the park for a nice photo op! How could you hate Denise after seeing those adorable kids having so much fun? Remember, nothing is sacred!

We never saw Ava Sambora out and about; we never even knew what she looked like. Then in March of 2008, Heather Locklear's shrink calls 911 thinking she may commit suicide. Oops! Then two weeks later, her ex-husband and father of her child, Richie Sambora, gets nabbed for a DUI with Ava in the car! Double oops! So what does the ultimate celebrity ex-couple do? They show off Ava, happy and smiling! All is well!

You can be skinny, you can be crazy, you can be a slut, or you can just have a baby! Having a baby is the least suicidal way to ensure hilton status. Find a baby daddy now! Someone famous, obviously!

Getting divorced?
Husband an asshole?
Take your kids out for
a stroll and show them
off to the paparazzi!

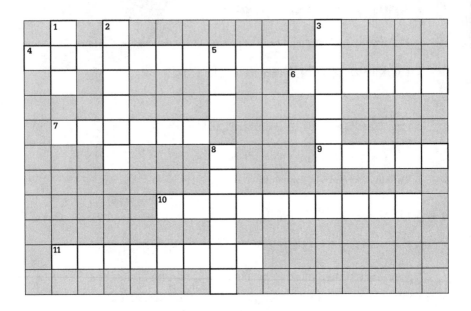

Across

4. Named after *Dragon Tales*?

6. Neil Young's imaginary friend

7. This ray can be ultra

9. "Of Sodom," for example

10. Town in New York state

11. Birthplace of Bushwick Bill
(of the Geto Boys)

Down

1. Romana, for example

2. Internet satirist

3. An inhospitable desert in
North Africa

5. Smart or Headroom

8. *The Platinum Blonde*

Across: 4. Max and Emme, 6. Shiloh, 7. Violet, 9. Apple, 10. Suri Cruise, 11. Kingston
Down: 1. Pax, 2. Maddox, 3. Zahara, 5. Max, 8. Harlow

STEP 8

I'm pretty now!

GET SOME WORK DONE

Not real work, silly. Plastic surgery! And since it's not 1986 anymore, it's time we redefine "plastic surgery." Plastic surgery used to mean you were a fifty-year-old woman going to an office on the Upper East Side of Manhattan to get a face-lift. Your husband was threatening to leave you, and you felt the need to fix the reason you were so unwanted: your face. It wasn't the fact that you stopped cooking dinner and having sex. So you went in and had the doc stretch your skin back a little, like a piece of plastic wrap. Hence "plastic" surgery. There's little or no actual plastic used, except to pay for the new, improved you!

Of course, rich women soon realized it wasn't only their faces that they wanted to restore. So they started getting their titties done. And don't forget dental work, hair plugs, butt implants, and anything else you might need. And after that? Labias!

Now Hollywood is full of nose jobs (paging Asslee Simpson, Jennifer Aniston, Tori Spelling!), face-lifts (hello, Cher!), thighs (Britney!), boobs (Vivica Fox, Posh, Sharon Osbourne, everyone else in town), vajayjay rejuvenation (paging Janice Dickinson, Rosanne Barr!), eye jobs (Katie Couric!), lips (Brittany Murphy! Lisa Rinna's have their own zip code!)—any body part you can think of. And the patients are getting younger and younger. Good-bye, Joan Rivers; hello, Ashley Tisdale!

Lisa Rinna's Lips

Since the surgeries exist, get them! No hilton would ever walk around fugs, especially when it's so easy to look hot. Let me walk you through some of the issues and procedures. Just think of me as someone who plays a doctor on TV:

- **KNOW WHETHER YOU NEED PLASTIC SURGERY:** It's pretty obvious—you're either fugs or not! Pamela Anderson is the perfect candidate *for* plastic surgery. Ever seen her without her makeup? She would look so much better if she had a little bit of work on the face to keep her looking hot. If a hilton starts to look old, she has to do something about it. Wrinkles and sagging skin do change people's perception of you, and with a little work, you can end up looking like a new, better person. Plastic surgery is a great thing, but a gamble! Remember Meg Ryan's face? She went from America's sweetheart to a plastic surgery cautionary tale! *Star* magazine put her on their cover with the headline, "WHAT HAPPENED TO MEG'S FACE?" Her lips suffered the most; she looked like she went twelve rounds with a boxing kangaroo! When you end up on the cover of magazines because you had bad work done, well, that's about as bad as you can screw up.

Since the surgeries exist, get them! No hilton would ever walk around fugs, especially when it's so easy to look hot.

PARIS'S NONSURGICAL ALTERNATIVE

Hang out with ugly people! Think back to when Nicole and Paris were really besties—Paris was this hot, skinny little number with long blond hair and Nicole was the chunky sidekick. Then Nicole got skinny, and Paris ditched her. Two years later, Paris was running with a "motor in the back of her Honda" nobody named Kim Kardashian. Then Kim got hot, got a sex tape, and got famous, and Paris was done, done, and on to the next one!

● **START WITH THE CHOMPERS:** Ever look at a hilton's smile? It's perfect and white. Go see a cosmetic dentist. Spend some money! This shit ain't free. (Unless you're a celebrity; then they gift it to you!) Veneers are really hot right now. Everyone's getting them, but let's call a spade a spade: Veneers are permanent dentures! You're no different from Grandpa if you get them! To give you veneers, the dentist files down your teeth and puts fake, porcelain-like chompers on top of your essentially now-destroyed teeth. It's *not* reversible. They file them down, demolishing your teeth and putting these fake teeth over them *forever.* You'd better be ready for the results, regardless of what they are— because there is no going back. If you don't like how they turned out, you have to get different veneers. Remember when Hilary Duff was this cute girl and then she got veneers, and it totally changed her face and her smile? She was criticized and had them redone. You don't want work done if it's noticeable. If you get veneers and everyone is talking about them, it's not a good thing.

- **GET THE JUGS DONE:** "Welcome to Hooters; may I take your order?" Face the facts—America loves a nice rack. So fix that problem now! It's not the eighties, and people aren't going to stare; they'll ask "Oh, wow, who'd you go to?" It doesn't matter whether you want smaller boobs, bigger boobs, perkier, more toned—whatever. If you've got floor-touching saggy boobs or you're flat like Kate Hudson, you've got to get them fixed. If a guy had an opportunity to go from a three-inch to a nine-inch dick, don't you think he would? *The Hills* reality star Heidi Montag did it for the sole reason that she thought she was flat. Well, guess what—she was! But she's not anymore. She had a lot of work done, including a nose job and her lips, and God knows what else. And she was only twenty-one! But she did what she wanted, and it obviously worked out. Salma Hayek had "the twins" done, but no one talks about it. If you get them done a normal size, it's like upgrading your car to a Ferrari. Destiny's Child singer Kelly Rowland got 'em done for the sole reason that she wanted to fit into this loose-fitting top she had bought! How awesome is that?

> Fourteen-year-olds don't need boob jobs! I have only one rule when it comes to getting work done: You should be at least old enough to vote.
>
> **PEREZ NOTE**

- **NEXT, THE HONKER:** Nose jobs used to be just something dorky teenage girls got done on a summer break before heading back to school. Now everyone gets them. They take, like, an hour to get done, and you're back in action by Monday. But you have to be careful; do I even have to bring up Ashley "the Nose" Tisdale? Quite possibly the worst nose job ever; she must be devastated. Or deviated. The best? Ashlee Simpson! Asslee is a perfect example of when plastic surgery goes terribly right. She was just Jessica's big-nosed younger sister, but now she's a gorgeous beauty who sells more records than Jessica! (Now if she could just work on that voice, supposedly being a "singer" and all.)

- **DON'T GO TOO FAR:** Look at Raquel Welch and Cher. Now, Raquel, she gets it right. She's almost seventy and she looks fucking amazing. She looks hotter now than she did when she was sixty! So obviously it's worth it, and it works for her. If you get plastic surgery to maintain your good looks, you want results like Raquel Welch has. You don't want to be in your sixties and look like Cher! I love her, but it's the awful truth. Cher is six years younger than Raquel Welch, and she looks like a freak frozen in time! That's an example of bad plastic surgery and too much of a good thing. I can't say for sure, but it *looks* like she had everything from a nose job, chin, cheeks, boobs, lips, and everything else worked on. She lost face trying to save her face. Kenny Rogers is another cautionary tale. He thought he had "lines around his eyes," so he went in for a quick fix-'er-up. He walked out of the surgeon's office looking like a different person, and he hates his new face! Can you imagine hating your new face? He looks so bad that now he's got to have surgery to correct his surgery! He should have known when to hold 'em.

THE JACKSONS

We can't talk about plastic surgery without mentioning the Jackson family. Michael's face is whiter than ivory, and it's melting and falling apart! If he's covered from head to toe, maybe he can go out and be normal. But then, by his being covered like a mummy, everyone will recognize him. La Toya's a complete mess, and Janet Jackson got a nose job and had her boobs done (they have a big indentation), at least. The funny thing is, the more work they have done, the more they all start looking like brothers and sisters again!

● **MAKE THEM WONDER IF YOU'VE HAD WORK DONE:** I sound like I'm contradicting myself, but I'm not. You don't want people to look at you and know instantly that you had something done, but you do want them to wonder what the hell you did to look so fabulous. One way to do that is with nonsurgical procedures. It's a Botox revolution, baby—men, women, and children! Madonna said she never got plastic surgery, but she's never said she hasn't gotten Botox. She's over fifty, and her face looks amazing. You know guys like Patrick Dempsey are popping in for a little fix-me-up. Britney herself was reported to get the lipo-dissolve. It's lipo without being lipo! What the hell does that mean? The doctor rubs a special wand over the cellulite and sends, like, lasers and waves through the skin to dissolve away the fat. Am I kidding you? No, I'm not! Guess what? I know another form of lipo without lipo: it's called a treadmill!

- **COME UP WITH A GOOD EXCUSE:** People may point at your new hot attributes and say, "She had work done," but you know what? They're right! You did have work done! That's why you are hotter than they are! All you need is a good excuse. Jen Aniston used the "deviated septum" excuse. Ashlee Tisdale? Deviated septum. Lance Bass, Ashley Simpson? Deviated septum! It's an epidemic. Cameron Diaz had her nose worked on, and she said a surfboard slammed into her nose and broke it while she was surfing in Hawaii. Perfectly plausible!

- **DECEIVE, INVEIGLE, AND OBFUSCATE:** If you can't come up with a good excuse, just lie. Never concede that you actually had your face changed. Has Nicole Kidman ever had work done? She's denied having Botox, but look at her. Her face is frozen like a Popsicle! I think Britney Spears had a boob job before she got megafamous (they were just too perfect!), and I think Jessica Simpson had a nose job early in her career and no one noticed it. On the other hand, Demi Moore admits to more than $400,000 worth of surgery. Doesn't that strike you as a little sad? A little mystery goes a long way.

SAFETY FIRST

After the death of Kanye West's mother, Donda, physicians and lawmakers have called for greater protections for patients undergoing cosmetic surgery. If Donda's Law is passed, doctors performing plastic surgery will be required to give patients full physicals before operating on them—something that Donda's niece says Dr. Jan Adams did not do.

Sure, a shrink will tell you that any problems you have with yourself physically are actually an internal problem you need to work out through years of talking in circles at $200 an hour. *Cough* bullshit *Cough* No amount of complaining will rid you of that hairy mole covering half your face! Do you want a lifetime of opening the door to a greeting of, "Hi, Aunt Mole!" Why would you learn to cope with a problem when you can just make it go away? To build character? That's for ugly people!

STEP 9

Grandpa

ROCK THE CRADLE OF LOVE

America loves its pretty young things. There were entire Web sites devoted to counting down to the Olsen Twins' eighteenth birthday, the age of legal consent, despite the fact that they look like chimps dressed as bag ladies. The Mickey Mouse Club cranked out nineties sex symbols Justin Timberlake, Britney

Spears, and Christina Aguilera—and now they have Miley Cyrus (whom Hugh Hefner has described as "welcomed in the magazine" upon turning eighteen) and the cast of *High School Musical*. If you're getting up there in the age bracket, dating a pretty young thing can vamp up your sex life, make people see you in a different light, and flat-out revitalize your worth in Hollywood.

TRUE HOLLYWOOD STORY

When I first moved to Los Angeles I temped as a receptionist at E! Networks, and one morning Janice Dickinson came in. She was pitching a show to the network, and we had a quick chat (i.e., I told her how obsessed I was with her). Then I complimented her on her gorgeous shoes, and she screamed out so everyone could hear her, "Do you know how many men I had to fuck to get these shoes?" Then she stormed off to go to the bathroom, stopped, and exclaimed, "Shit! I forgot my tampon!" As if! That bitch stopped ovulating twenty years ago! Anyway, she made a total scene of the fact that she was "fucking guys" and still "using tampons." She wasn't really, but she gave everyone that impression, because she knew it made her seem younger and hotter. Anyway, I blogged about it that night, and needless to say, E! Networks saw it and asked me not to come back. Oh, well!

take a dip in the fountain of youth

You can't just go out and ask Zac Efron if he'd like you to seduce him and then expect people to forget your true age.

There's the right way to appear younger than you are, and there's the wrong way. The right way is to take a dip in the fountain of youth and find someone *slightly* younger than you, someone who makes you *feel* young. Someone you can run around with on the beach in Saint-Tropez, while the paparazzi snap you in your thong bikini and your ripped young lover in his nut-hugger Speedo. Someone who bangs you a few times a day like you haven't been banged since your Studio 54 days, and in return, you buy him a Porsche. It's a fair trade, and it's the way it's done.

Rank the Cradle Robbers

On the list below, rank the couples from greatest to least age difference:

___ A. Céline Dion and René Angélil

___ B. Hayden Panettiere and Milo Ventimiglia

___ C. Madonna and Guy Ritchie

___ D. Demi and Ashton

___ E. Tom Cruise and Katie Holmes

___ F. Woody Allen and Soon-Yi Previn

___ G. Catherine Zeta-Jones and Michael Douglas

___ H. Nick Cannon and Mariah Carey

___ I. Harrison Ford and Calista Flockhart

Answer Key: 1F (35 years), **2A** (26 years), **3G** (25 years), **4I** (22 years), **5E** (16 years), **6D** (15 years), **7B** (12 years), **8H** (10.5 years), **9C** (10 years)

do it the right way

Madonna finally ruled the world, as she had promised Dick Clark she would back in 1983. She got married, got divorced, fooled around with Warren Beatty, Dennis Rodman, and Vanilla Ice, had kids, and in the end realized she needed to settle down. Her Madgesty dipped into the fountain of youth to find a young, strapping hubby with star power of his own to keep her satisfied. Madonna and Guy Ritchie have a ten-year age difference, but you have to hand it to her: She is in really good shape. Where was she going to find a fifty-year-old man who could handle that action?

My favorite May/December couple has to be "Halo," Hayden Panettiere and Milo Ventimiglia. He's thirty and she's eighteen, and they know it's pervy, because they sneak around everywhere and took forever to acknowledge they were dating. What are they hiding? They should call him Milo Pedophilia! Can you imagine being a senior in high school and banging some thirty-year-old dude? I can, and it's hot!

Demi and Ashton have got Madonna and Guy Ritchie beat—theirs is a fifteen-year age difference. Old enough to pee, old enough for Demi! When he's forty, she'll be fifty-five. I guess he didn't want to have kids! Of course, he's got three already; he's got Demi's kids—Scout, Tallulah, and Potato Head. They call Ashton "MOD"—"my other dad." I call him "F.A.G." But you have to hand it to them: They are by *far* the most famous of the May/December relationships, even though they are only number six on "Rank the Cradle Robbers." They somehow spun a semi-retard banging an elephant-kneed has-been into some kind of cougar female-empowerment movement. Well played!

Don't forget Tom Cruise and Katie Holmes and their sixteen-year age difference. No one ever picks on them, but the age difference for Tom and Katie is larger than Demi and Ashton's. Katie was eight years old when Tom was starring in *Top Gun*! How is that not pervy? Go figure.

Harrison Ford is looking pretty good for someone in his sixties (I'd do him). He's twenty-two years older than Calista Flockhart, but I'm *sure* they're having a good time. I wonder if he uses his whip on her? "Oh, Indy!"

29

48

Old enough to pee. old enough for Demi !

Hugh Hefner was supposedly banging three different young hotties at once: Holly, Kendra, and Bridget. I have serious doubts that he actually had sex with these women; the man is 150 years old. Even with Viagra, he'd just have a heart attack if he tried anything more athletic than pitting prunes. Maybe he keeps a gimp in the grotto to satisfy them? But of course it doesn't matter, because he's selling a fantasy, and having three girls whose ages add up to a number that is *still* half your age is ingeniously hilton.

don't do it the wrong way

Usually when there's a huge age difference between two hil-tons, the gossips go crazy and write everything they can about them. It's great, free publicity! Geena Davis and husband Reza Jarrahy have a fifteen-year age difference, but it's one of those instances where being in a May/December relationship *doesn't* get you written about. Why? Because she didn't date *up*! Nobody cares about Katharine McPhee and Nick Cokas and their nineteen-year difference. Honestly, I have nothing to say except, "You're a loser from *American Idol,* and your husband is nineteen years too old."

Catherine Zeta-Jones and Michael Douglas have a twenty-five-year age difference. When they first got together, they were the talk of the town! She was a newbie on the Hollywood scene, and he was a dinosaur. The fact that he landed her was good gossip. In all seriousness, they've managed to last a long time, so sometimes it does work out! Of course, now that they've lasted, they're boring and B-list. All they do is live in Bermuda and do nothing.

Céline Dion and husband René practically started dating the day she was born. She was thirteen years old when he began working with her, and they claim it was ten years later that she first planted a kiss on him. Surrreeee!!!! He is twenty-six years older than she is! Ewwwww. That's the same number of years between Rod Stewart and Penny Lancaster, as well. I don't even want to think about her having to keep his rod forever young, but at least she is collecting a lot of pennies for her trouble.

The absolute worst has to be Woody Allen and Soon-Yi Previn, a thirty-five-year age difference. She's young enough to be his daughter! Oh, wait, for a time, she was!

> **If you're getting up there in the age bracket, dating a pretty young thing can vamp up your sex life . . .**

especially don't do it the very wrong way

In June of 2002, R. Kelly was arrested on twenty-one counts of child pornography after he allegedly had sex with and video-taped a fourteen-year-old girl sometime between November 1997 and February 1998. *Perv!!* Of course, prior to that, Kelly had settled lawsuits with two other women who accused him of having sex with them when they were minors. And don't forget he married Aaliyah, his former protégée, when she was just fifteen! In 1977, at age forty-four, Roman Polanski had to flee to France to avoid sentencing for unlawful sexual intercourse with a minor, specifically a thirteen-year-old girl he plied with champagne, quaaludes, and private photo shoots. Please step awayyyyyy from the children!

stay forever young

Not all celebrities are out there having insane, swinging-from-the-chandeliers sex with some young thang. Some are having old, dry, crusty sex. Tom Hanks and Rita Wilson, for example. I think they are happy, but I don't care about them.

When a true hilton gets old, there's still that need to get nailed in night vision. One day, sooner than she thinks, a hilton will be a MILF, and eventually a GILF. As Janice Dickinson wisely teaches us, sex keeps you young, and staying young is essential in Hollywood. Dating someone younger is the perfect way to maintain a pulse, both in life and in the public eye. You don't want to be tossed into the graveyard like Meg Ryan, Al Pacino, Melanie Griffith, Sharon Stone, and the rest of the over-forty-five group who can't get a good role to save their lives.

PRETEND TO GIVE BACK

Not everything you do to become a hilton has to drag down all of society with it. Most of it, yes, but not all. You could look at it as a glass-half-full type of thing—like the less food you eat, the more there is for starving people. Or the more things you buy, the better off the economy will be. And

> Charity without press
> coverage is like peeing
> yourself in black pants:
> It gives you a nice,
> warm feeling, but no
> one really notices.

there's always the *mandatory* public service after getting a DUI, so a hilton will inevitably help out the community, whether she likes it or not.

It's not hard to get blitzed and start swerving across the yellow lines of a highway, and anyone can hole up in a four-star hotel to do a bag of blow and get banged all night on camera. But surely there is the road less traveled? I bring it up every once in a while on my site: the positive things a hilton can do. Every once in a while, even a hilton answers the call of duty and at least pretends to give back to the community, whether it's charity, the arts, or the cause du jour.

I'm not saying that no celebrities are earnest. Jenny McCarthy fights for new laws and studies with regards to autism, a condition that her son lives with. But if you're going to be a hilton, just make sure that whenever *you* show up for a charity, you know where the cameras are. Charity without press coverage is like peeing yourself in black pants: It gives you a nice, warm feeling, but no one really notices. Angelina Jolie's going to donate the sale of baby Shiloh's pictures to charity? Make sure it ends up on the cover of *People*! Jessica Simpson's going to Iraq to visit the troops? Cover of *GQ*! And it goes without saying that the accommodations must be five-star and first-class, so that it's worth your while!

One holiday season, Spencer Pratt was photographed giving Thanksgiving food to the poor. But guess what? It's Spencer

Pratt! We *know* you're an asshole, Spencer. You were pretending to lend a helping hand to get press, and the only thing you were thankful for was the paparazzi.

give back to your family

You think Jessica Simpson thought to sell her jugs to the world all on her own? No! Papa Joe was there for her. Dad Joe Simpson was instrumental in creating her image, getting her on *Newlyweds* with Nick Lachey, and subsequently ruining their relationship. Then he did it again with sister Ashlee!

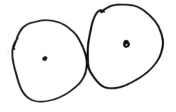

Miley Cyrus has her mom and her dad working for her. Britney? Mom and Dad. Lindsay and Ali have mom Dina. Usher uses his mom as his manager. The Duff sisters use their mom. Beyoncé's dad runs her career.

See a trend? They're all gorgeous and young and flaunted their sexuality to make it big. Britney, Jessica, Miley, Lindsay— we've seen about 98 percent of their bodies, and in some cases (Britney, Lindsay), we've seen as much as their gynecologists. It was their parents who put them out there for us, but as they say, Father knows breast. Fifteen points on the back end is the least a child can do to thank her momager for giving her public life.

do some work

That's right! Get up and do something. It will blow everyone's mind, and some people even say it's a source of satisfaction or something. Anyway, at least it's a break from the all-too-repetitive average day in the life of a hilton, which is:

- **EIGHT A.M.**—Get up and put on my 7 For All Mankind Jeans and Gucci tank. Get in Range Rover and head out to Starbucks. Tired of Coffee Bean. Order a venti—no, make it a tall; I gotta cut back on carbs—soy latte to drink on the way to gym.

- **NINE A.M. TO ELEVEN A.M.**—Work out with trainer. Drink a protein shake. Look in the mirror. Arrange photo op (i.e., have paparazzi waiting outside gym for when I come out looking all buff) and call agent and let them know I'll be at the Ivy for lunch.

- **ONE P.M.**—Lunch at the Ivy with my agent. Hopefully he brings along someone hot for fun. Wear new Marc Jacobs V-neck showing off chest and tan.

- **FOUR P.M.**—Yoga. Fuck, what do I do from three p.m. to four p.m.? Fuck, I gotta find something to do. Maybe I'll call my mom? No, I did that last month.

- **SIX P.M.**—Watch TV and see if anyone is talking about me.

- **EIGHT P.M.**—Start getting ready. Maybe have a stylist come over and pick out some clothes for me and do my hair. If she's hot, maybe I'll bang her.

- **NINE P.M.**—Walk the red carpet at a premiere for someone else's movie (I haven't worked in months). Don't actually stay to watch movie.

- **NINE FIFTEEN P.M.**—Dinner at the Ivy. I don't know if enough photographers got me at lunch.

- **ELEVEN P.M.**—Party at Foxtail. Or Villa. Or Goa. Fuck, which place is hotter? Call Paris. Find out which place is hot. Maybe it's Winston's.

- **TWELVE A.M.**—Move to another bar

- **ONE A.M.**—Booty-call that hot waiter from the Chateau Marmont. Have sex.

- **TWO A.M.**—Get some sleep.

- **FOUR A.M.**—Get up to pee. Wow, I drank way too much. Go back to sleep.

- **EIGHT A.M.**—Get up and put on my 7 For All Mankind Jeans, Gucci tank. Get in Range Rover and head out to Starbucks. Tired of Coffee Bean. Order a venti—no, make it a tall; I gotta cut back on carbs—soy latte to drink on the way to gym.

Take a break from the all-too-repetitive average day in the life of a hilton . . .

Even though she created the hilton image, the one thing you can't say about Paris is that she's lazy. She's up early in the morning and late at night, being Paris Hilton. Ryan Seacrest is on *American Idol*, his own radio show, and his own TV news show on E!—he's nonstop. Simon Cowell has three shows on TV: *X Factor, Britain's Got Talent*, and *American Idol*. He's also got his record label Syco music.

He hustles, and, all kidding aside, I love the hustlers. Even Nicole Richie had to not eat for a *long time* to make scary skinny happen!

hire *a* friendsistant

Keep your "friendsistant" close, but your "frienemy" closer. Jessica Simpson's Cacee Cobb is probably the most famous friendsistant of them all. They were best friends; then one day Cacee just started working for her! Trace Ayala was Justin Timberlake's good friend. Then he became the assistant; then he got upgraded to business partner. Bringing your friend on board to work with you is like opening up a whole new life for them of VIP access, money, sex, and fame! (Note to self: They should make a show about that; HBO would be perfect.) On the downside, Tejano superstar Selena was shot in the back by her friendsistant, Yolanda Saldivar, so it's not without risks.

hire *all* your friendsistants

A hilton needs an entourage, because being alone is like saying no one likes you, no one follows you, and no one wants to roll with you. Whether they are going shopping, going out to dinner, heading to the tanning salon, or going to bed, a *real* hilton is never by herself. She's always got her entourage with her. Think about it; when was the last time you saw Nicole Richie, Paris Hilton, or Lindsay Lohan by herself? They are always with someone else, and it's always someone less famous than they are—an assistant, a security guard, a scruffy friend, a DUFF (designated ugly fat friend), or a gay. It's certainly not someone who will steal the spotlight.

Remember, Nicole Richie had a falling-out with her wannabe-celebrity-stylist Rachel Zoe when Rachel herself started wearing all of the fabulous clothes, posing on the red carpet, giving quotes to the media, doing interviews, and acting like a celebrity!

Having a big entourage can draw a lot of attention to you and make you look like a big diva. At the 2006 VMAs, Diddy rolled onto the red carpet with an entourage of ten people—everyone from his record-label peeps to his assistant, friends, security, and business acquaintances. Bella Capricorn, Diddy's personal assistant, said, "Getting Diddy here takes a small village, a lot of hotness, and a mirror." Having a big entourage is a status symbol, like driving a big car, because it's not as though the people in your entourage come free. Hairdressers, stylists, and personal trainers cost money, especially if you want to fly them all around the world. While most members of an entourage supposedly serve the purpose of making sure their boss looks camera-ready and hot as can be (like touching up makeup or fixing a loose shoulder strap), they seem to be doing double duty keeping their star company. When you don't have real friends, buy some!

Don't get me wrong; I totally get it. If you've got millions of dollars to burn, and part of your moneymaking ability is

A hilton needs an entourage, because being alone is like saying no one likes you, no one follows you, and no one wants to roll with you.

dependent on looking and feeling good, you need your glam squad to travel with you. You need your trainer by your side shouting, "Don't eat that! You'll have to do a hundred and fifty sit-ups if you eat that! Don't drink that! That's four miles you'll have to run to burn off just one of those!" Rain or humidity could mess up your 'do, so you've *got* to keep a hairdresser close by! Of course, trainers and hairdressers don't fetch you drinks and cigarettes and point out cute boys and listen to you bitch and moan all night, so you need your assistant/slave with you *at all times*—ready to answer your call, no matter the hour. In-N-Out Burger at three a.m.? On it! Who else is going to put up with that? And don't forget the bodyguard, in case someone tries to mug you and take your wallet (never mind that your assistant is probably carrying it for you). And a driver, so you don't have to drive, unless your publicist recommends another DUI.

But these are just the basics, so you should feel free to be inventive, as many of the great hiltons have done. For example, in the allegedly severe stages of a rumored eating disorder, Mary-Kate Olsen was said to have a meal minder, whom she called an "eating coach." I can see this coach now: "C'mon, Mary-Kate! You can do it! Lift the fork, c'mon, go, go, go! Awwww! Good try. We'll give it another shot a little later." Remember when Katie Holmes had a Scientology friend and assistant? In the early days of dating Tom, Katie had her Scientology friend Jessica Rodriguez accompany her everywhere she went. I guess once they fully indoctrinated Katie, there was no need to follow her around anymore. I wonder what the fuck happened to her minder since then? Where does that job lead to next, MK-ULTRA? Lindsay had a "sober companion" when she left rehab center Cirque Lodge in 2007. These new minders are people who are there with a hilton to prevent them from doing what they *really* want to do.

An entourage doesn't have to always be made up of assistants and hairdressers. Sometimes they are family, like when Britney's dad pretty much babysat her after her meltdown. Sometimes they are your loser buddies, like when rappers think they are hot shit because they have an entourage twenty or thirty people deep, consisting of all their old friends from the neighborhood. Many celebrities, especially those who've been burned a lot in the past either by the media or gossip or bad relationships, feel safe around their entourage and need them. They become shut-ins or become weary of making new friends or have trust issues, so it always comes back to their peeps!

Jen Aniston's hairdresser, Chris McMillan, gave her more than just the "Rachel" cut; he gave her his loyalty. They're BFFs, and he'll never leave her, unlike *some* people! She was even rumored to have moved in with him after her troubles with Brad (though her rep denied it). She calls her publicist, Stephen Huvane, one of her besties, as well. Hey, maybe there's something to that—having all of your best friends work for you, and having all of the people who work for you be your best friends!

They were the first to deny Eva Longoria's pregnancy, they set her up with her soul mate, and they were her shoulders to cry on: yup, the hairdresser and the stylist. On several occasions back in '08, Eva's stylist, Robert Verdi, denied publicly that Eva was pregnant: "I'm not her gynecologist, but I am her stylist," he said. "I see her naked. I see her boobs! That's the first place it would show, and it's not showing!" When rumors surfaced that her hubby, Tony Parker, had cheated on her, Eva ran to Ken Paves, her hairdresser, showing up at the opening of his new salon. Eva is also best friends with Liza Anderson, who is referred to as her "friend and publicist."

Jessica Simpson loves her "mane man" Ken Paves so much, she started a company with him, doing a line of hair extensions called HairDo. Everyone knows that Ken is the man in Jessica's life—no matter whom she is dating! Of course, don't forget she is always best friends with her stylist, and, of course, her assistant (who for the longest time was her best friend, Cacee Cobb). Plus, Jessica has her sister and the rest of her family, so with an entourage like that, who needs friends?

From assistants to bodyguards to agents to family members, Britney always seems to be surrounded by her team. Whether it's manager Larry Rudolph, an assistant/cousin (her longtime assistant–turned–best friend Alli Sims is actually a distant cousin), the paparazzi (Adnan), her mother, an agent (she went to Mexico with agent Jason Trawick), her father, brother, bodyguard, or "the manny," Britney's friends and employees have become indistinguishable. Of course, I use the term *friend* liberally.

Lindsay's best friend? Jenni Muro, her assistant! But here's a case where it makes sense. Lindsay's had so many people rat her out and so much bad shit happen to her over the years that she *needs* her best friend to be her assistant, or more so her assistant to be her best friend. When have you ever seen Lindsay alone? Even in rehab, she ended up shacking up with a boy, Riley Giles. She has always had a boyfriend and/or girlfriend, and she is rarely spotted without some hanger-on walking two feet behind her.

Mariah Carey could be the biggest entourage diva ever! Personal umbrella holders, trainers flown in from the Caribbean—she's got it all! She's rumored to have shown up to the VH1 Save the Music 10th Anniversary Gala with nine assistants. What did she need nine for? One of the assistants handled the brushes and hair spray, one dealt with the hot rollers, one had the breast tape, and the rest were probably security, publicity, drink fresheners, and who knows what else! She supposedly had an entourage of fifty when she showed up at Pure in Las Vegas after one of her concerts, and she even had her own personal deejay, DJ Suss. One, spinning for her.

Brad and Angelina have a ton of security, rumored to cost millions per year—and they need it. They've got six kids, and look what happened recently: Their people got in a nasty fight with a paparazzo who was dressed in camouflage and moving in on their property in France. Could you imagine spotting this gossip commando doing a Rambo crawl toward your house full of young children? So for them, I'm all for it. Add to the list Brad's mom, who was in France helping out, as well as Angelina's brother, who was there also. It's like a circus, but they need the help! I don't know how many are on their team, but if you count family, friends, bodyguards, staff, travel people, assistants, publicists, and more, I'm sure Team Jolie-Pitt runs fifty deep! That's basically a corporation!

Matthew McConaughey had a hair colorist, makeup artist, personal assistant, trainer, and personal chef on the set of his film *Sahara*—an entourage that reportedly cost over $500,000.

The perks of being A-list! Yay for Mateo. If you can get that, go for it.

Hollywood stars are always trying to outdo their peers with silly things like who has the biggest trailer. And why not? We know Hollywood is built on excess, and one of those excesses is a massive caravan of royal servants. Hiltons have too many people doing too many things for them, which is why they start to lose it as they get older—they've never done anything for themselves! Now make my ice water colder, bitch!

pretend to go green

Have a team of stylists and makeup artists and bodyguards go everywhere with you, and use up a massive amount of resources on a daily basis. Then make sure to say, "Oh, I drive a Prius," or, "I don't drink bottled water," as you step from your private jet onto the tarmac, twenty Louis Vuitton trunks in tow. Whether you're driving hybrid cars, covering your mansion with solar panels, or wiping your million-dollar ass with one square of toilet paper (use both sides!), make an effort to publicly show we can all make a difference.

Never hesitate to tell everyone you're green, because there are different kinds of green: eco-friendly green, green you can smoke, and, of course, the almighty green dollar.

You can say you're "green" while sitting in your air-conditioned dressing room, drinking bottled water, and wearing a fur suit made by toddlers in a sweatshop—so long as you're toking a joint and getting paid $10 million for this movie, that's *very* green!

Does this mean hiltons are hypocrites? Yes, but so is everyone else—as *Us Weekly* says, "Stars . . . they're just like us!"

Cameron Diaz, Tom Hanks, Susan Sarandon, and Tim Robbins were among the stars who pulled up to the 2003 Academy Awards in hybrids and electric vehicles instead of limos. It's not like they are out on the highway picking up trash—when they are supporting a cause, they make sure there is a press release, and a lot of cameras. But that's what celebrities are for: to get attention! "Going green" may be a worthy cause, but to me, green is the new AIDS. In the nineties, it was all about AIDS, but Hollywood seems to be pushing for the environment now. It is the latest trend, like gladiator sandals.

Leonardo DiCaprio has a green house, a green apartment, and solar panels on his home; drives a hybrid car; and the Leonardo DiCaprio Foundation has fostered awareness of environmental issues in cooperation with many environmental charities. But even Leo has his scorched-earth moments. In 2006, he reportedly flew his family from Paris to Rome on a private jet *and* declined a journalist's challenge that he never fly private again. Chris Martin has been known to fly home after gigs—sometimes thousands of miles—just to relax a bit before going back on tour. But he plants mango trees all across the planet to even out his massive amounts of travel! Celebrities are like politicians—they all lie, and the fun is, we get to catch them with blogs and cameras! Laurie David, who brags about using recycled toilet paper and who, for the love of God, produced *An Inconvenient Truth,* says to those who point out that she flies on a private jet that "what hurts the environmental movement [is] holding people to a standard they cannot meet." Fuck, not flying on a private jet is a standard I meet every day!

Leo DiCaprio says he tries to fly commercial "as often as possible." How come I find it possible every time I fly?

Hayden Panettiere is into saving the whales and dolphins. She, along with six other activists, paddled out on surfboards in Japan to stop a dolphin hunt in 2007. The fishermen started poking them with poles. Hayden was seen breaking down into tears on camera speaking about it. Dolphins are her thing, but "cause" aside, she *needed* to do this. Her image was squeaky-clean; then all of a sudden she's dating an older guy (and getting poked with *his* pole). And though she's supposed to be the goody-goody, she's been photographed hanging out with Paris Hilton and dancing on stripper poles and smoking cigarettes. Her dolphin cause evens it all out and makes her seem like she's wise beyond her years. In 2006, Daryl Hannah sat for three weeks forty feet above the ground in a large walnut tree to protest the planned demolition of Los Angeles's South Central Urban Garden. Talk about making a splash with a fish-out-of-water story!

By donating $5 million of his own cash to help build green homes, Brad Pitt is helping to rebuild the Lower Ninth Ward in New Orleans, which was ravaged by Hurricane Katrina. Every $150,000 makes sure that a family gets a new eco-friendly and disaster-proof home. Like hope, they even float! Brad's into "green," but when was the last time he flew commercial? It seems like his entire life is spent on his private jets going from country to country, not to mention the fact that he and Angelina have got to bring all of their kids around the world with them. And whenever they land, they've got their massive security teams along with them in giant SUVs. But could you imagine seeing the entire Brangelina clan on an AirTran flight

red carpet suicide

to New Orleans? The kids would be fighting over the peanuts, Maddox would be grabbing the stewardess's ass, and everyone would be trying to take pictures and bothering them. Brad Pitt also announced he will be a design consultant for a hotel and resort Zabeel Properties plans to build in Dubai that will feature "environmentally friendly architecture." In Dubai . . . the only country in the world that impacts the environment more per capita than we do in the U.S.? Where they build indoor ski slopes because they are *that* rich and can afford not to give a fuck *that* much?

Barbra Streisand was called out by the British press for traveling by private jet, while an entourage of fourteen crew and band buses, several vans, a private limo, and thirteen trucks hauled her crap. This after her Web site tells us to "wait until you have a full load before running your dishwasher" and to "turn off lights when not in use and *dim lights when in use*" (emphasis mine). She reportedly asked for 120 bath towels on her rider upon arrival at a concert, and there's also a rumor that she spends over $20,000 a year to keep her lawn looking green—but oops, Babs, that's the wrong kind of green! And supposedly her twelve-thousand-square-foot barn is air-conditioned. Barbra is a diva—that's who she is, and she wouldn't be Babs if she didn't live like that!

See, it's complicated being a hilton. By using the attention you attracted with your self-indulgent consumption, you're expected to warn the world about the dangers of self-indulgent consumption, all while not looking like a complete douche bag hypocrite . . . somehow.

detoxify

After a lifetime of physical and spiritual toxicity, a true hilton finds ever newer, faster, and more mystically effortless ways to cleanse herself. And once she tries something new, she shares it with everyday people by staking her claim to it and appropriating it into her own fame. Have you ever heard of anyone else doing "cupping" before or after Gwyneth Paltrow did it? Has anyone tried "leech therapy" since Demi Moore? Who is the first person you think of when you think of kabbalah? What about Scientology? Celebrities have found a new way to expand their brands—detoxifying the mind, body, and spirit with their own various personal practices. And they are *happy* to share their methods with you, as long as you don't forget who pioneered each one!

Gwyneth must have really wanted the toxins out of her body, stat, because she didn't fuck around. While some people drink a lot of water or sit in a sauna, Gwyneth went with a treatment where you create suction by lighting an alcohol-soaked cotton ball in a cup; then you place the cup on your skin. The skin gets sucked up and rises under the cup as blood rushes up to the surface. It's supposed to improve circulation and help with menstrual cramps and digestive problems. Of course, what cupping *really* does is leave big circular cup marks all over your

a true hilton finds ever newer, faster, and more mystically effortless ways to cleanse herself.

back, so that when you walk around in public showing them off, the tabloids go crazy with speculation. Is it a tropical disease? Is she being abused? That's what Gwyneth did in 2004, and it was a brilliant stunt.

Just before the summer of 2008, Oprah Winfrey said good-bye to hot dogs, hamburgers, and BBQ with her twenty-one-day vegan detox plan. She also laid off the caffeine, sugar, gluten, and alcohol. And, of course, just to make sure everyone knew all about it, Oprah blogged her every move. It's hilarious, because unlike cupping, vegans are common. In LA, you can't swing a Slim Jim without putting out a vegan's eye. Somehow, by limiting her commitment to twenty-one days and adding the word *detox,* it's like Oprah was the new face of veganism. Veganism is Oprah's thing, *because she just doesn't commit to it.* She is the master.

In 2008, Demi Moore told David Letterman that she uses bloodsucking leeches to "cleanse" and "detoxify." Granny Demi visited a spa in Austria that offers it as part of their services. The "highly trained medical leeches" attach themselves to you and detoxify your blood, and she thinks it is so effective that she's going back for more! I guess the queen of the cougars will do anything to keep up with her plaything, Ashton Kutcher. You know what I think? I think the leeches are for her a stepping-stone to full-on vampirism.

find religion

Madonna has been involved in the spiritual movement of kabbalah (rooted in Jewish mysticism) for over a decade now.

She's even written songs about it, such as "Ray of Light"—it's like she's a cantor! And don't forget the $26 red string bracelet—said to deflect "envious stares and looks of ill will." (And I thought showing off that you can afford to throw away $26 on a piece of string was the *cause* of envy and ill will.) As we've come to expect from Madonna, she's not keeping the religion to herself. She's introduced everyone from Britney Spears to David and Victoria Beckham, Demi and Ashton, some of the girls from *The Hills*—and of course her hubby, Guy Ritchie. (Maybe she ties him down with red string before they have dirty religious sex!) Roseanne Barr says kabbalah is the force behind her own rejuvenation; maybe it also inspired her revagination? Kabbalah may have been around for thousands of years, but it was just collecting dust before Madonna came along. She should get a percentage of whatever they make per year, like half! Kabbalah is big business, and it would be nothing without her. At the same time, the more it catches on, the more her name gets mentioned by association—smart!

Tom Cruise is Scientology's Madonna. Tom probably spends more time on Scientology than anything else, and I don't think that doing anything excessively is a good thing. All of the videos leaked of him being crazy—they just make him look bad. I think he's too deep in it. It's his number one priority. Twenty years from now, when he's in his sixties, he'll probably not be as hot an actor then, and he'll have more time on his hands, so he'll probably be the new church leader. That's my prediction. P.S.—Don't forget the rumors that Scientology cures homosexuality. I knew this one guy who joined and he stopped being gay. True story. Maybe it'll work for Tom!

serve in public office

Become a mayor like Sonny Bono or Clint Eastwood, a congressman like Cooter from *Dukes of Hazzard,* or a governor like Arnold or Jesse Ventura. Or you can go all the way like Ronald Reagan—become the president! Anything is possible for a Hollywood celebrity, especially one with a few monkey pictures on his résumé.

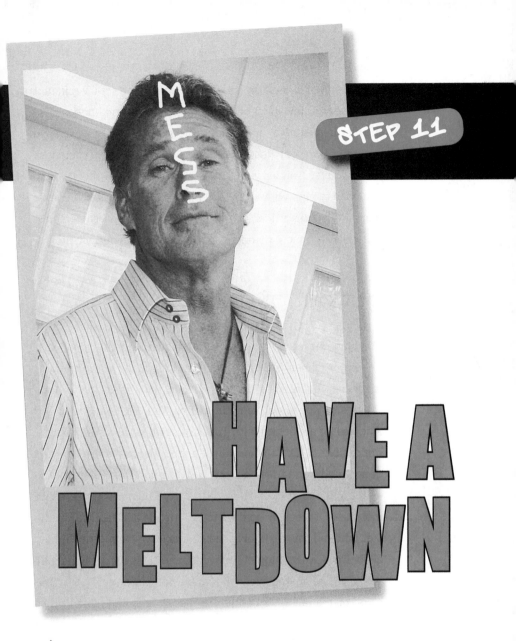

STEP 11

HAVE A MELTDOWN

Any soccer mom can realize it's time to lay off the white zin, or that she wants to switch from pharmaceutical sales to real estate and also get a divorce. She might join a support group, sign up for a class at the Learning Annex, have an affair on eHarmony, or lose herself collecting Hummel figurines. When a hilton hits rock-bottom, it's a totally different kind of event, involving police escorts, viral Internet videos, fleeing the hemisphere, and scaring the shit out of Oprah. You've got to shave your head, eat a hamburger through your nose on YouTube, wander into a stranger's house, and then kidnap someone to burn with your crack pipe. Having a meltdown never helped anyone's career, but it is a hilton rite of passage, and it will make you more notorious in the annals of celebrity history.

get out of dodge

The smoothest kind of celebrity meltdown is just to *poof* disappear. It makes you mysterious, and if you leave the country, it makes you seem a little like Jason Bourne. In 2005, Katie Holmes disappeared. Sometime after April 11, she flew to Los Angeles for a meeting with Tom Cruise about a role in *Mission: Impossible III*. For sixteen days, nobody knew where she had gone, and by the time she returned, she had fired her longtime agent and manager. In June 2007, Foxy Brown disappeared for more than a week, according to her friends and family. But the star who did this meltdown the best is Dave Chappelle. In May 2005, Dave was on top of the world, and then suddenly nobody knew where in the world he was—not his agent, his publicists, or his fans. He had just signed a headline-making deal

When a hilton hits rock-bottom,
it's a totally different kind of event,
involving police escorts, viral Internet
videos, fleeing the hemisphere, and
scaring the shit out of Oprah.

with Comedy Central for two years at $55 million. Rumors flew around that he was a crackhead, he had spent all the money, or that he was in the loony bin. Later we learned that he was on the other side of the world, taking a "spiritual retreat" in South Africa. It turns out he was just getting his head together. But when he announced that he was walking away from his $55 million deal, we all wondered why this man *wasn't* in the loony bin! Now he lives just outside of Yellow Springs, Ohio, on what he calls Fuck You Hollywood Farm.

In a way, none of these celebrities really did this meltdown right, so the category is still open for the killer application. Foxy nobody really missed—bitch *crazy*. Katie we still miss, because she came back as some sort of Stepford zombie whom everybody feels uneasy about. And Dave, he never really came back. He's off polishing the clock in Town Square with his shirt-sleeve, thinking it's 1903. Open casting call for this one.

cry like a bitch

In late 2007, Heather Mills broke down in tears as she revealed in an interview with Britain's GMTV that she's tired of the "eighteen months of abuse" from the media. Poor hooker with a heart of gold! Getting $48.7 million plus payments of $70,000 per year is even more than the $20,000 a night she alleg-edly used to make as an escort. Even the cops are sick of her shit—the chief superintendent of the Sussex police compares "a disproportionate high volume of calls from Heather Mills McCartney" to the boy who cried wolf. The *Sun* wrote what should probably be this woman's epitaph: "Hooker, Liar, Porn Star, Fantasist, Trouble Maker, Shoplifter." Completely distraught and with tears rolling down her cheeks, she told her interviewer that she feels like she's being made to look like a monster. You'd think somebody poured a jug of water over her head! She's a good actress, so I don't think she is being honest when she has her meltdowns. She's complaining about the same media she was using herself, because without the media, she'd be nothing. No one was forcing her to read the newspapers or watch TV, but a narcissist like Heather eats it all up. She loves it—she lives for it. Madonna doesn't read or watch this stuff. She purposely chooses not to. But we know Madonna's got a leg up on Heather!

The video of Paris Hilton crying on her way to jail was a top Web video hit. Like Heather Mills, Paris deserved her punishment, but unlike Heather Mills, people felt sorry for her. She's like a golden retriever, and you know that you have to smack her on the nose with a newspaper, but you feel terrible doing it. She says she learned a lesson, but she has the memory of a goldfish. Even though I keep using animal metaphors here, I think this meltdown made her more human.

On January 7, 2008, Hillary Clinton cried like a bitch when asked, "Who does your hair?" A lot of people thought it was a transparently calculated move by a frosty candidate, but that has *got* to be a genuinely touchy subject with her. Anyway, was it really a meltdown? Maybe more like a thaw.

If you're going to cry, I'd say do it like Paris. Have a pretty good reason, like jail ("abuse by the tabloids" doesn't cut it),

> **If you're going to cry, I'd say do it like Paris. Have a pretty good reason, like jail . . .**

and don't seem like your tears are those of a conniving opportunist—it shouldn't be completely obvious how you hope to benefit from them.

go viral

In May 2007, a video of David Hasselhoff, reportedly taken by one of his kids, surfaced online showing him incoherent, crawling on the floor, and stuffing his face with a Wendy's hamburger. Shortly after the video circulated, he stated, "Because of my honest and positive relationship with my children, who were concerned for my well-being, there was a tape made when I had a relapse to show me what I was like." The Hoff also issued a statement saying that the clip was released deliberately. Okay, but deliberately by whom? I can buy that he agreed to make the tape as a way of looking in the mirror, but which one of you little shits sent it to TMZ? Haven't you ever heard of "Don't Hassle the Hoff"? And what's the appropriate grounding for international public humiliation? Unfortunately, the tactic didn't work, and since the video, he has been hospitalized for alcohol poisoning. I think it embarrassed him, but it didn't save him. He's got a serious problem he has chosen not to get serious help for. Somehow, against all common sense, the Teflon Hoff was awarded full legal custody of his two girls on June 15, 2007, a month after the video went public.

After his daughter didn't answer a prearranged call at the home of his ex-wife, Kim Basinger, Alec Baldwin cussed out the eleven-year-old in a voice mail. Media everywhere ran the message in which Alec is heard calling his daughter a "rude, thoughtless little pig." He got a ton of flak for this, but some people were glad somebody had the stones to call it like it is: Tween girls are a complete nuisance with their phones. At least one Web site nominated him for Father of the Year.

Viral video meltdowns don't seem to have hurt either Alec Baldwin (who is beloved on *30 Rock*) or Hasselhoff (who got custody of his daughters). In both cases, they got a ton of attention, and we forgive them for making the kinds of mistakes we all have made—and being unlucky enough to see it aired all over the world. On the other hand, when the November 17, 2006, video of Michael Richards throwing out the n-word seven times while doing stand-up at LA's Laugh Factory went viral, you could just see the guy's career ending before your eyes. That's a good example of what not to do.

make yourself at home

On August 19, 2000, Anne Heche knocked on the door of a stranger's home in Cantua Creek, California. She was scantily clad and seemed out of it when she claimed her car had broken down. She requested a shower and then got comfy. She asked for a pair of slippers and suggested they watch a movie, but didn't call any friends or a tow truck. When the cops arrived a little later, Anne announced that she was God and would take everyone to heaven in her spaceship. Robert Downey Jr. got even cozier in May of 1996. While under the influence of a controlled substance, he trespassed into a neighbor's home and fell asleep in one of the beds. You know what, though? I can think of worse surprises than finding Robert Downey Jr. in my bed.

get caught stealing

On December 12, 2001, Winona Ryder was arrested for shoplifting $6,000 worth of clothes and accessories from the Beverly Hills Saks Fifth Avenue. She got a ton of publicity and three years' probation. Later that month, on December 27, Martha Stewart upped the ante by selling her stock in Imclone Systems on an illegal tip from her broker. This move saved her about $50,000 but cost her five months in jail. But neither theft can hold a candle to the bad boy of funk, Rick James, who stole a twenty-four-year-old woman. During a cocaine binge in 1991, Rick held Frances Alley hostage for six days, tied her up, forced her to perform sexual acts, and burned her with his crack pipe. And that, ladies and gentlemen, is how a hilton melts *down*! Cocaine is a hell of a drug!

REACH OUT AND ASSAULT SOMEONE

September 1998: Naomi Campbell assaults assistant Georgina Galanis with a telephone.

March 2005: Naomi Campbell beats assistant Amanda Brack with a BlackBerry.

June 2005: Russell Crowe throws a cell phone at a Mercer Hotel employee.

March 2006: Naomi Campbell throws a jewel-encrusted cell phone at housekeeper Ana Scolavino.

give them a run for their money

If there is a more exciting meltdown than a celebrity police chase, I don't even want to know about it. In 1988, James Brown delivered the goods as few hiltons do. He led cops on a PCP-fueled car chase from South Carolina to Georgia with a shotgun on the passenger seat. When he tried to run over the cops and they shot out his tires, he drove on flat tires until the wheels fell apart. You're welcome to try, but I don't think you're going to top that.

On June 17, 1994, O.J. Simpson led LA police on an hour-long low-speed chase in a white Bronco driven by his friend Al Cowlings. After an hour of driving and an hour of negotiation, O.J. surrendered. He's no James Brown.

I honestly can't give any advice when we have James Brown's perfect example of a police chase celebrity meltdown. Just copy him as exactly as you can manage, right down to the crooked wig.

jump the couch

Inspired by the *Happy Days* episode that signaled the beginning of the end for the series, "jump the shark" has come to refer to anything so over-the-top that there's nowhere left to go. Inspired by Tom Cruise, "jump the couch" has a similar meaning: to go so batshit crazy that no one knows how to deal with you. In May 2005, Tom appeared on *Oprah* and professed his love for Katie Holmes by jumping on Oprah's guest couch, shaking and wrestling the most powerful woman in television, and literally dragging Katie Holmes out from backstage. Oprah thought he'd lost his mind completely and told Tom repeatedly, "You are gone!" This stunt totally backfired. Tom, no matter how real or honestly he was behaving, showed us a little too much of a Tom Cruise we weren't used to. For whatever reason, in August 2006, Paramount Pictures declined to renew their production contract with Cruise. He had a 40 percent drop in his popularity and was voted the celebrity people would least like as their best friend. Sometimes, you just gotta chill when things aren't going right! On the other hand, Tom Cruise was the only thing anyone could talk about for the rest of the year. He's not as out of control anymore. Maybe Katie punished him, and now he's not allowed to act like that. Suri throws the tantrums now.

Britney Spears "jumped the couch" by shaving off all her hair at a San Fernando Valley salon in February 2007, and then again in January 2008, when she barricaded herself in her bathroom, reportedly half-naked, with son Jayden until a police escort took her to the Cedars-Sinai Medical Center psych ward. At the height of her craziness, Britney Spears was at her most popular. My numbers went up through the roof, because everyone wanted to watch. It was epic—

> If there is a more exciting meltdown than a celebrity police chase, I don't even want to know about it.

the downfall of America's golden girl. You couldn't have scripted 90 percent of what happened, it was so unbelievable. Mariah Carey went nuts on MTV'S *TRL* in July 2001. She gave out Popsicles from a pushcart and then began a striptease for no reason. She told Carson Daly, "I just want one day off when I can go swimming and eat ice cream and look at rainbows." She was soon hospitalized for that epidemic unique to celebrities, "extreme exhaustion."

SHOW ME THE RECEIPTS!

In late November of 2001, Whitney Houston performed on Michael Jackson's two-hour CBS special. She looked like such a crackhead mess in the performance photos that everyone thought she must be on drugs, anorexic, bulimic, or all of the above. About a year later, she did an interview with Diane Sawyer and explained that the most infamous photo was just "a bad shot." When asked about drugs, she jumped the couch: "Crack is wack. If I do crack, show me the receipts!" How effing crazy do you have to be to think that if Diane Sawyer doesn't have *receipts* for your *crack*, it proves you are innocent?

Imagine if we had cameras always following Tom Cruise, Paris, Paula Abdul, and Heather Mills—we would see meltdowns and insanity times twenty times worse than we have seen. I can't even imagine half the stuff Heather Mills does and the conversations she has in real life. I would love it if they were secretly videotaped or recorded. That's why public meltdowns are so cherished, because they are the few moments we get to peek inside the mind of a celebrity for that one second when they absolutely lose control.

R.I.P.

JUST DIE ALREADY

Real hiltons leave the world with a thunderous bang of dramatic tragedy, and they wouldn't be caught dead just dying in their beds at eighty-three. That won't get anyone talking about "what could have been." Get it done, and get it done early, James Dean style. Look how famous and iconic James Dean became, and *how many movies did he actually make?* In your death, you should try to combine as many of the following factors as you can:

- Drugs
- Sports cars
- Suicide
- Autoerotic asphyxiation
- Murder
- Private aircraft
- Cult leaders
- Yachts
- Bloods and Crips
- Paparazzi
- Royal conspiracy
- Vomit
- Nudity
- The toilet

You could be as worthless as Brody Jenner, but so long as you choke on an OxyContin in the crapper of your G5, all of Hollywood will come out to praise your life and genius:

"He was so devoted to his craft."

"He was such a great person."

"His creativity will be missed forever."

You will be missed? Yeah, by your dealer! By your enablers and handlers and hangers-on! When a hilton dies, the artistry lies in how easily it could have been avoided. Tom Hanks and Rita Wilson are still alive, but only because they are not high on coke, giving head at 120 mph in a Lamborghini! Zzzzz . . .

A HILTON SALUTE TO THOMAS CRAPPER

Where would hiltons be without the modern toilet? It's where they vomit their meals, dry-heave after a bender, snort their drugs, have sex with strangers at the club, and, often enough, it's where they ultimately kick the slop bucket. Thomas Crapper was the key figure in the invention of the modern toilet, holding nine patents, including the floating ball cock. It also owes a debt to Alexander Cummings, who took Crapper's ball cock to its climax. You ever hear of "praying to the porcelain god"? Crapper actually stamped his toilets with this branding: "The Venerable Crapper." It's like he just *knew*! To learn more, see Wallace Reyburn's 1969 book *Flushed with Pride: The Story of Thomas Crapper.*

don't fail at failure

Owen Wilson, Britney Spears, Heather Locklear—there have been so many "almosts" in recent years. Owen was rushed to the hospital for an apparent attempted suicide. Britney was strapped onto a gurney and hospitalized against her will. Talk about drama! Heather Locklear's shrink thought she was going to kill herself and called 911. These failed attempts at tragedy will get you press, but so will winning a Razzie for "Worst

Actor"—and they're both as chic as socks with sandals. Here are some more losers who couldn't even fail properly:

- Adam Ant
- Billy Joel
- Brian Wilson
- Brigitte Bardot
- Clark Gable
- Danny Bonaduce
- Diana, Princess of Wales
- Donna Summer
- Drew Barrymore
- Drew Carey
- Elizabeth Taylor
- Elton John
- Eminem
- Gary Coleman
- Greg Louganis

- Halle Berry
- Hank Williams Jr.
- Johnny Cash
- Marianne Faithfull
- Mike Wallace
- Ozzy Osbourne
- Patty Duke
- Richard Pryor
- Sammy Davis Jr.
- Sid Vicious
- Sinéad O'Connor
- Tina Turner
- Vanilla Ice
- Walt Disney

Family will only get in the way. They'll try to stop you from achieving true hilton status.

red carpet suicide

keep your relatives far, far away

Owen Wilson, Britney Spears, Heath Ledger—where were their families during their tumultuous times? Far away! Everyone knows that if you're in trouble, your friends and family should step in and help you! Even the ones who aren't fucked up keep their families away. Jennifer Aniston doesn't talk to her own mother! Hell, she's rumored to talk to Brad Pitt's mom more than she does her own! Drew Barrymore was estranged from both parents, Halle Berry from her mother, Eminem from both parents, Angelina Jolie from her father, Lindsay Lohan from her father, Amy Winehouse from her mother, Courtney Love from both parents, Demi Moore from her mother, Sharon Osbourne from her father, Christina Aguilera from her father, Meg Ryan from her mother, Dr. Laura Schlessinger from her mother, Anna Nicole Smith from both parents, Britney Spears from her mother, and Tori Spelling from both parents. Family will only get in the way. They'll try to stop you from achieving true hilton status.

THE WORST PARENTS IN AMERICA?

Sure, Paris, Nicky, and Barron Hilton are still alive, but good Lord, the Hiltons must be the worst parents in the world. Paris got a DUI, Barron got a DUI, and Nicky may be anorexic. A trifecta!

do not go gentle into that good night

Heath Ledger's death was by far one of the saddest tragedies to hit the entertainment world in a long time. But there's a great lesson to be learned: If you want to be a hilton, don't end up old in a nursing home. Instead, get naked and have your unlicensed masseuse find you on the bed after an alleged overdose. If the first person she calls upon finding your limp body is your secret lover (Mary-Kate Olsen would be ideal), then all the better! Then watch from the beyond as the secrets about your life surface posthumously: the lovers you had, your secret torments, the drugs, the money problems. How come your agent could never find a script this good?

Why did all of America put on a big, distraught show over the "passing" of Anna Nicole Smith? She was a total slut with fake boobs who used to be a stripper, posed naked in *Playboy,* had two kids out of wedlock, did massive amounts of drugs, married a dying eighty-year-old man for money, exploited herself and her family on a reality show, and was a nuisance to society for the last decade of her life. She was awesome!

And that's why we celebrated her. That's why her death was a

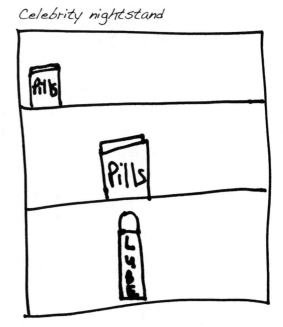

Celebrity nightstand

media event that rocked the U.S. for weeks, if not months. She did everything right, on schedule, and according to plan. Did she not sell out her baby to the press? Did she not get scary skinny (thank you, Trimspa!)? Did she not date up (a dying billionaire)? Did she not do massive amounts of drugs? Did she not drink like a pirate? Did she not have a ton of sex, with all kinds of crazy partners? She spent at least two years on a downward spiral, and her every move brought her one step closer to the grave. Slurred speech, less clothing, revealing intimate secrets, many lovers, trips to the hospital, extreme weight loss, crazy interviews—it was all happening right in front of us! We watched the train wreck, and we gave her show great ratings! She stuck to the playbook and then went out in style, a model hilton to the end. She pushed it as far as she could. Anna Nicole couldn't have done it any better, and she is a shining beacon for us all.

throw away a long, happy life

You can't starve yourself, do massive amounts of drugs, sleep with hundreds of different partners, drive fast cars, put yourself in dangerous positions, live gluttonously and selfishly, and then still expect to live a long, happy life. Let other people suffer through life's most precious moments: watching their children graduate and marry, celebrating their golden anniversaries, and looking into the eyes of their grandkids and even great-grandkids. Who would even want these things? The ugly, the poor, and the unpopular, that's who!

You can't starve yourself, do massive amounts of drugs, sleep with hundreds of different partners, drive fast cars, put yourself in dangerous positions, live gluttonously and selfishly, and then still expect to live a long, happy life.

Test Your Skill

On the list below, fill in the age at which each star died:

___ Jimi Hendrix

___ Robert Johnson

___ Brian Jones

___ Janis Joplin

___ Jim Morrison

___ Jean-Michel Basquiat

___ Kurt Cobain

Answer key: A 27, B 27, C 27, D 27, E 27, F 27, G 27

EARLY EXIT
MAD LIBS

_____ , one of the world's brightest young stars,
CELEBRITY

died today in _____ in _____ . The
IMMEDIATE LOCATION   GEOGRAPHICAL LOCATION

cause of death was announced as _____ . This beloved
NOUN

figure was only _____ years old.
NUMERAL

Jayne Mansfield:

a Buick Electra • Slidell, Louisiana • chauffeur error • 34

Buddy Holly:

a Beechcraft Bonanza • Clear Lake, Iowa • "Big Bopper" fibbing about weight, pilot error • 22

Ritchie Valens:

a Beechcraft Bonanza • Clear Lake, Iowa • coin toss • 17

James Dean:

his Porsche 550 Spyder • Cholame, California • turnipseed error • 24

Marilyn Monroe:

her bed, naked • Brentwood, California • the Kennedys • 36

Jimi Hendrix:

a Samarkand Hotel room • London • vomit error • 27

Jean Harlow:
her room • a Los Angeles hospital • scarlet-headed fever •
26

Robert Johnson:
a country crossroads • Greenwood, Mississippi • whiskey
poisoned by a jealous husband • 27

River Phoenix:
a spot outside the Viper Room • Los Angeles • being "too
conscious," and also a speedball • 23

Anna Nicole Smith:
her Hard Rock Hotel and Casino room • Hollywood, Florida
• eleven drugs and spices • 39

Keith Moon:
in the same room in which Cass Elliot had died four years
earlier • London • the six pills in his body that had dis-
solved, of thirty-two total • 32

Bob Marley:
Cedars of Lebanon Hospital • Miami • Rasta no abide
amputation • 36

Sharon Tate:
her home • Los Angeles • sixteen stabs by Charles
Manson's disciples (Manson murdered *up*!) • 26

Janis Joplin:
her room • the Landmark Motor Hotel • not-so-cheap
thrills • 27

John F. Kennedy Jr.:

his Piper Saratoga • the Atlantic Ocean • pilot error, curse
• 38

Elvis:

the venerable crapper • Graceland • none—Elvis lives • 42

Razzle:

Vince Neil's DeTomaso Pantera • Los Angeles • beer run
• 24

Joe C.:

his parents' house • Taylor, Michigan • three-foot-nine-
inch frame could not accommodate ten-foot dick • 26

Otis Redding:

a chartered plane • Madison, Wisconsin • plane sittin' on
the bed of the lake • 26

Edie Sedgwick:

her home • Santa Barbara • Santa Barbiturates • 28

DJ Screw

the bathroom of his studio • Houston • purple drank • 29

Jim Morrison:

the tub • a Paris apartment • hot bath • 27

Hank Williams:

a Cadillac • Oak Hill, West Virginia • B12 shot (with mor-
phine) • 29

Bruce Lee:

Betty Ting Pei's apartment • Hong Kong • five thunder-
bolts of the Triad Society • 32

Brandon Lee:

a scene from *The Crow* • Wilmington, North Carolina •
prop gun, curse • 28

Natalie Wood:

earshot of her yacht • the Pacific Ocean off of Catalina
Island • drowning, intoxication, laid-back attitude of rescuers
• 43

John Lennon:

front of the Dakota • New York • extremely fickle auto-
graph seeker • 40

Jesus of Nazareth:

Golgotha • Iudaea Province • our sins • 33

Princess Diana:

a hired Mercedes-Benz S280 • Paris • royal conspiracy,
candle burned out long before (legend ever did) • 36

Kurt Cobain:

the greenhouse above his garage • Seattle • Courtney
Love • 27

Joan of Arc:

the Vieux Marché • Rouen, France • Deuteronomy 22:5
• 19

Sid Vicious:

his girlfriend's house • New York City • curiously strong heroin • 21

Ian Curtis:

his kitchen • Macclesfield, England • the chicken wouldn't stop • 23

Aaliyah:

a Cessna 402 • the Bahamas • too much luggage • 22

Selena:

a hospital • Corpus Christi • friendsistant • 23

Tupac Shakur:

Suge Knight's BMW 750i sedan • Las Vegas • thug life • 25

Notorious B.I.G.:

a GMC Suburban • Los Angeles • beef • 24

Brian Jones:

his swimming pool • Sussex, England • misadventure (British) • 27

Bon Scott:

a friend's car • London • misadventure (British) • 33

John Belushi:

bungalow 3 • the Chateau Marmont • involuntary manslaughter by speedball • 33

Chris Farley:

his apartment • Chicago • speedball, idol worship • 33

Lord Byron:

Messolonghi • Greece • fever, leeches • 36

Nick Drake:

his home • Tanworth in Arden, Warwickshire •
Melancholy, amitriptyline • 26

Heath Ledger:

his loft apartment, face down and naked, waiting for his
masseuse • SoHo • oxycodone, hydrocodone, diazepam,
temazepam, alprazolam, doxylamine, idol worship • 28

Your Name Here:

_____ • _____ • _____ •
_____

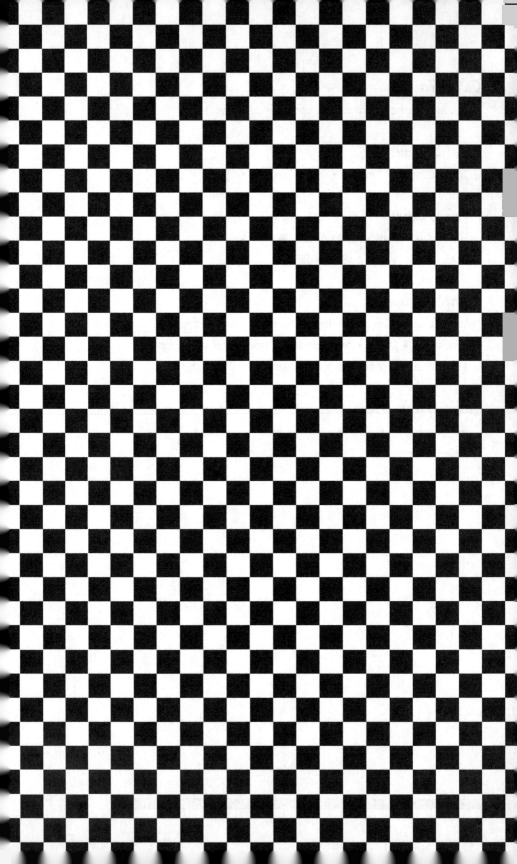

★ *Part 2* ★

THE FUTURE OF HILTON

In the $future,$ hiltons will live in San Bernardino after LA falls into the ocean, all red carpets will be green, and game shows and reality television will be the standard. The biggest reality shows will be *America's Next Top Hooker, Project Runaway,* and *So You Think You Can Exotic Dance.* Grand Theft Auto XXVI will revolutionize gaming by actually giving you herpes. Actors will have worn out their welcome after too many strikes, so all movies will be CGI, even documentaries. There won't be any musicians, except folk musicians, because file sharing has made the profession less profitable than subway busking. All fashion will be crotchless, and gossip headlines will be reserved for A-list celebrities who die in only the most spectacular ways, like getting strapped to a rocket and blasted into the sun, or drinking whiskey poisoned by a jealous husband. And every celebrity will have a last name that we're already familiar with today, because Hollywood is an incestuous town.

Celebrities all date one another, and we'll start to see their children date one another's children. Since they date only other famous people, it's a tiny dating pool, kind of like dating only within your church. While most parents in America are trying to get their kids to hang out on the playground with kids whose parents are doctors and lawyers, in Hollywood, you want your kids to hang out with other famous kids. Do you really think Tom and Katie will be leaving Suri in a Van Nuys apartment complex sandbox for a playdate?

In Hollywood, you want your kids to hang out with other famous kids.

Granted, a lot of parents do try to give their kids normal lives. Pam Anderson is always spotted at her kids' soccer games (but she brings a new date to each one!). Tom and Katie were always cheering on son Connor during soccer season, but I don't see too many of these kids going on to earn athletic scholarships. Mostly, what the middle-aged stars' kids are doing today is . . . well, trying to break into Hollywood. But they missed the boat. The Rumer Willises of the world are just living off of their parents' names. They can't all be the next Kate Hudson and represent the new generation of Goldie Hawn. The rest of these clowns aren't going to have that kind of luck. Their destiny? I can't imagine there's going to be too much artistic success there. They could always go the "famous for being famous" route, like Lionel Richie's li'l gal Nicole. How's that album coming along, Nicole?

Now, take someone like Colin Hanks, son of Tom Hanks. He's an adorable actor and handling his career smartly. He's not out partying every night and just trying to be a big movie star. He's acting, taking it slow, getting some roles, and living his life. Rumer desperately wanted to be famous, not to be an actress. In her head, she was probably saying to herself, *I'll just be an actress, because it's an easy way to be famous.* For her, she's thinking at least it gives her a job, and she thinks instead of being a party girl, she can be a working actress who likes to party. Only it hasn't worked out that way, because she tried to be famous before getting a career. She started to get fame very early, first by being the daughter of Bruce Willis and Demi Moore, and then by being friends with other famous girls (who don't hang out with her anymore). She leeched onto Lindsay

Lohan very early on. She was photographed with Lindsay walking in and out of the clubs. Then when that was over, she latched onto Hayden Panettiere. She attached herself to other girls to make herself famous before she was even twenty-one years old. For every Rumer Willis, there are probably two or three children of celebs who have managed to live under the radar, who don't party and go to premieres—but she's the one who gets all of the attention.

Rumer Willis aside, the real stars of tomorrow are part of the new crew of youngsters: Lourdes, Maddox, Shiloh, Zahara, and Pax Jolie-Pitt, Kingston Rossdale. These are the kids who are going to own Hollywood. Not Rumer "Potato Head" Willis. She doesn't have the look, and she doesn't have the talent.

The interesting thing about celebrity culture and stars is that once you achieve a certain level of fame, you will always be famous. Once you crack A-list and even B-list, you can sustain it for the rest of your career. I use the career of Sharon Stone or Demi Moore as a perfect example of that. Neither of those two has had a hit in over a decade, yet they are just as famous today as they were ten or fifteen years ago. Whether we like it or not, Lindsay Lohan will always be famous. If she was famous in 2004, she'll be famous in 2020 (dead or alive!). And it doesn't matter what she'll be famous for—it probably won't be movies—she will be doing QVC by then—but she will be famous. Even Tara Reid will still be famous.

> **Once you crack A-list and even B-list, you can sustain it for the rest of your career.**

One day, Madonna's daughter, Lourdes, will grow up to be the biggest pop star on the planet. She's famous now for being Madonna's daughter, but her star will only shine brighter. Angelina's kids will be the coolest in school, the Olsens will get pregnant, Paris will get married—it will never end! Lindsay Lohan will have a child. It'll be a new crop of troublemakers driving drunk down Sunset Blvd, making sex tapes, posing nude on the Web—step aside, Miley Cyrus; Harlow's here and she means business!

I mean, really, do we think Suri is going to grow up and go to business school? Is Kingston Rossdale going to scrub in for brain surgery? Can you picture Shiloh running her own venture capital firm? We know where these kids are going—straight to Hyde, Bungalow 8, and the Palms. These kids are destined for stardom. They've already got 90 percent of what it takes to be a superstar in Hollywood: good looks, money, a name, and a stylish wardrobe. Maddox and Kingston have already donned the mohawk hairdos; Suri's been spotted in everything from Burberry to Marc Jacobs. Most of them have already been on the cover of all of the major magazines out there. Popularity will *not* be an issue. When these tykes turn sixteen years old, every auto maker with a publicist will be banging down their door to deliver them any car they want:

Dear Maddox,

From all of us here at General Motors, please accept this Cadillac Escalade hybrid as a special sweet sixteen birthday present. Drive safe!

Sincerely,
Rick Wagoner, CEO
GM

In fact, they'll probably give him a different color for every country he visits while touring the world with his mom and siblings!

See, these little hilton kids are commodities. Cadillac, Burberry, Nike—they'll all want to be branding these little munchkins, because as they get older, their product choices will be all over *Vogue, Life & Style, The View,* and PerezHilton.com! These kids are big business.

And they'll all create such great romance, drama, and even their own children in the future! I wouldn't be surprised if Shiloh Jolie-Pitt at some point dates Kingston Rossdale. Their parents (Brad and Angelina and Gavin and Gwen) are friends and hang out. So it would be more than appropriate; it's even expected. I wouldn't be surprised if little Harlow fucking hates Benji and Paris's kid, if they have one. They will be the cousins who don't get along. Hollywood is a cycle. There will always be villains and angels, druggies and saints, actors and freeloaders.

While much of the future I'm painting here looks good, a lot of future hiltons are headed down a dark path. These kids are inheriting more than just good looks from their parents—they're inheriting the propensities for DUIs and jail, divorce and illegitimate children, eating disorders, drugs, alcohol, fights, and plastic surgery. They get the addiction gene, the ego gene, the bad-attitude gene, and the fast-car gene. Are they just going to turn it all down? Maybe. Both of the Lohan sisters chose the path of stardom, while their brothers decided to go academic. It doesn't always mean you *have* to be famous, just because you are born into it. All of Donald Trump's children

See, these little hilton kids are commodities.

sweat it out in the corporate grind. They could easily marry wealthy and live off of either set of parents' moola.

ANGELINA'S KIDS:

What if Angelina's kids all go back to their respective countries and change the world as we know it? Her dreams will have come true. I don't see Angelina's kids just smoking pot and going to house parties in the Hollywood Hills. They will make a difference and live life to the fullest. I don't think they'll have the tendency to rebel either. They will rebel with their parents naturally by doing cool and fun adventurous things normal kids will never get to do growing up—like live in a zillion-dollar French château! Maddox already wears a mohawk. If he's feeling wild, he'll dye his hair pink. He'll wake up and just do things like that. He's already had color in his hair—most kids' parents wouldn't let them do that. I see them all doing good for the world.

Most likely, though, the future stars of Hollywood currently burning up the playgrounds will end up assuming the various roles their parents and predecessors occupied decades before. There will always be a need for gossip and drama, there will always be partyers in Hollywood, and some guy eventually will come in and sweep li'l Harlow Madden off her feet. And maybe even get her preggers!

Until this batch of little munchkins grows up, we're stuck with "talent" like Spencer Pratt and Heidi Montag. Hurry up, Lourdes; grow a rack! We need some other people to look at! Think about it, if Rumer Willis were hot and dating, say, Zac Efron, she'd be a star! People would give a shit, and we wouldn't have to look at Heidi and Spencer. But until then . . . we'll just have to wait and suffer.

pereznac the magnificent's predictions

Shiloh—I would imagine Brad and Angelina probably want her to go to college. She will be like her nickname, "Shi," and won't want the spotlight. Of course, she might also be anorexic, since her mom used to refer to her as a "blob."

Maddox—I see him actually being a daredevil of sorts. I can see him racing motorbikes or being a stuntman. He's really into racing and guns and violence. I see him doing something action-packed and dangerous. Maybe even traveling the world and competing with Dad Pitt after he retires from acting.

Zahara—She's a little attention whore. She loves the camera and is ready for her day in the spotlight. Ultimately, I see her returning to Africa as an ambassador.

Pax—He'll probably be the least successful. He was adopted when he was older, and they are the forgotten ones, usually.

Twins Vivienne and Knox—They'll probably be drug addicts. Both of them, like Redmond and Tatum

O'Neal. We know their mom had an issue with drugs in the past—that shit doesn't just go away!

Violet Affleck—I see Violet being a big movie star. She loves the cameras in a good way. She's always smiling for the paparazzi. I see her being the next Reese Witherspoon or Julia Roberts. She'll be doing big romantic comedies, always smiling, chasing boys. I think she is a very happy, normal kid. They try to make life normal for her. Either that or she's just well trained for the cameras! Anyway, she'll do some coming-of-age movies in her teens, then find that big-time *Legally Blonde* or *Pretty Woman* role that launches her into a new stratosphere. And when she gets nominated for her first Oscar, old Ben and Jen will be clapping in the front row—white hair and all.

Kingston Rossdale—He'll definitely join a band. That's what you do if both of your parents are musicians. Definitely not a solo artist—he's a band kind of boy, a little rocker. He's maybe the most stylish, too. Kingston Rossdale will be the badass of Hollywood, but he won't ever get into trouble. His parents wouldn't let him.

Sean Preston Federline—If I were Sean Preston I'd write a book called *After the Darkness*. Of course, in his case, we just hope he knows how to read and write. But you've got to think that the things that he saw his mom, Britney Spears, do and go through, then living in dad Kevin Federline's house, would make for a hell of a tell-all!

Jayden James Federline—Britney went through a pretty tough time in the days leading up to and after his birth. I just hope he makes it to eighteen and runs the fuck away. I see him opening up a motorcycle shop and maybe a garage. He'll drive a Harley!

Apple and Moses Martin— Their parents, Chris Martin and Gwyneth Paltrow, hate the paparazzi and celebrity media frenzy. So the same shit will happen with Apple and Moses, and they will grow up miserable. I see nothing from them. They will live in the U.K., and no one will care about them. End of story!

Harlow Richie-Madden—I see her definitely getting arrested as a teenager. She'll be a troubled teen, and then she'll turn her life around. Like mother, like daughter. But I hope she keeps eating—she's really thriving!

While much of the future I'm painting here looks good, a lot of future hiltons are headed down a dark path. These kids are inheriting more than just good looks from their parents—they're inheriting the propensities for DUIs and jail, divorce and illegitimate children, eating disorders, drugs, alcohol, fights, and plastic surgery.

Suri—Scientology's first female leader! All hail the queen! She'll probably teach at the Scientology center. Just what Tom always wanted!

JLo and Marc Anthony's Twins Max and Emme—I hope they get her butt! I see them working the family business—working mom's fashion business.

JLo's got millions invested in her brand, and the kids will take over!

Isabella and Connor Cruise—They will move to London and live with Apple and Moses, and no one will care. Suri will get all of the attention, just like now!

Liam "Spelling"—I hope he gets some of Grandpa's money. His mom didn't. I see him getting plastic surgery like all Spellings do as teenagers. Nose job at sixteen. Pecs enlarged at eighteen. Maybe some face work, new calves . . . followed by a reality show on public access television. I wonder if he'll ever be upset at his mom for constantly selling his baby photos to the tabloids for money?

Max Bratman—He'll be a behind-the-scenes music manager like his dad, Jordan; then he'll become an accountant. Maybe he'll keep breast-feeding off mom Christina till he's eighteen!

Denise Richards's Kids—Well, technically they're half Charlie Sheen's kids, too. I see them murdering their parents, though! And tipping off the paparazzi that they're doing it. They'll be the next Menendez siblings! We'll all be riveted by the trial.

Pam and Tommy's Kids—I wonder if they've ever Googled their mom? I'm sure the kids at school have shown them the infamous Pam and Tommy sex tape. They will probably work as porn directors. It runs in the family! They'll have learned from the best.

YEARBOOK AWARDS

Most Likely to Get a DUI: Harlow Madden. It's going to be tough for her parents to curb any bad habits. She was born within less than a year of Nicole's major problems—drugs, alcohol, DUIs! I hope they don't push Harlow's carriage the wrong way down the street!

Most Likely to Be a Slut: Paris and Benji's kid! She'll be flashing all of the kids in kindergarten: "Hey, look at me—no diapers!"

Most Likely to Be a Reality Star: Liam "Spelling" on public access. Tori and Dean got their show on the Oxygen network, but Liam won't be so lucky.

Most Likely to Record a Hit Album: Kingston Rossdale. It will be a cross between his dad's rock and his mom's pop.

Most Likely to Be a Designer: Suri! She won't really need the money from being a Scientology teacher—she'll just be doing it to fit into the family business. But Suri has been a fashionista since she was two years old. She'll be creating waves with her fashion at the mere age of ten, when she rocks a circa-2002 look on the red carpet for her dad's fiftieth anniversary of *Risky Business*. By her late teens, she'll be known for her new line of dresses called "LRH" (named after Scientology founder, L. Ron Hubbard).

Most Likely to Be Frienemies: Harlow and Benji and Paris's kids. Their parents hated each other and loved each other all at the same time! So will the kiddies!

Sunday Rose Kidman Urban—She'll be a doctor . . . just because. I have a feeling she'll be raised very properly, and when she's a doctor, she can treat her father when he goes back in for rehab!

Honor Marie Warren—Jessica Alba's career will be over in five years, so I think they will be living in Oklahoma, because it's cheaper and they'll be broke. Honor Marie can open up a Mexican restaurant just to piss off her mom, or better yet, she'll make Jessica work there and finally get in touch with her Latin heritage.

people who shouldn't procreate

Hollywood loves sex and loves making babies. Everyone from a teenage Jamie Lynn Spears to an unwed Nicole Richie is popping them out. But while some moms and dads in Hollywood are totally fit to raise their kids right, others need to start doubling up on birth control. Four people who should have all baby-making rights stripped from them are:

Charlie Sheen shouldn't have any more kids. And Denise Richards either. Neither together nor with others. They've done such a bad job with their current kids, they don't need any more.

Larry Birkhead doesn't need to have any more kids. One is enough to whore out. Dannielynn made him a lot of money—not only by inheriting Anna Nicole Smith's fortune, but also from his selling the kid out to magazines and TV shows!

Lindsay Lohan will be the worst parent. You pass on what you learn from your parents, and both of her parents are messes.

> Hollywood loves sex and loves making babies.

what will happen to our favorites?

Imagine Paris as a senior citizen—she'll be like the new Jack Nicholson! She'll take vacations, go where she's popular (Europe, South of France), she'll have a young boyfriend like Ivana Trump does. She'll just keep partying until the sun goes down . . . or she does!

Nicole Richie—she will be really fat in her old age. You can maintain that level of extreme thinness for only so long. It can't be forever. Her body will rebel for torturing it as long as she has. She'll eat the early-bird specials at Denny's and IHOP, and her metabolism will slow down. She'll weigh almost 180 pounds! OMG!

Tara Reid—she will be the oldest stripper in Vegas, her destiny fulfilled.

Lindsay Lohan—she'll be dead, sadly.

red carpet suicide

Miley Cyrus—she'll be another B-minus-list star like Hilary Duff has become. She'll be able to transition to some extent, but her light won't shine as brightly.

Spencer and Heidi—they will still be on reality television, because they love it! They are good at it!

Jesse Metcalfe—he'll be a gardener in real life by then.

Pam Anderson—she'll be the new Joan Rivers, getting plastic surgery nonstop, and hawking hair extensions on QVC.

The Olsens—there won't be interest in their fashion lines or DVDs anymore, so they'll be living off their hundreds of millions. To keep busy, they'll be, like, playing cabaret shows on the gay circuit.

Britney Spears—she'll probably be dead. There are just too many forces against her to hope for a long-term future. Is she going to spend the rest of her life under someone else's control? She hates being under someone's control, but she's got a mental illness, and she'll either be controlled by someone in her family (like her dad) or by a boyfriend or bad influence (like Adnan!). Either way, I don't see her lasting. I believe she came pretty close to the stripper pole in the sky the last time she hit rock-bottom. The next time, she may not be so lucky.

Zac Efron—he's going to get Vanessa Hudgens pregnant to prove he's not gay! Of course, if she does get pregnant, he should demand a paternity test. It's not like the old days, back when you could trust the integrity of a chick with naked photos all over the Internet.

Jessica Simpson and Ashlee Simpson—

divorce! Both of them. Jessica, of course, we know is capable of some divorce. Her first marriage with Nick Lachey ended in divorce, and every relationship since has ended in a headline: "SPLIT!" She's sort of known for being the girl who can't hold down a steady BF. (When Nick asked if he could get a hummer on *Newlyweds,* she said, "You mean the car?") As for Asslee, she and Pete are very cute together, but at some point that act will wear off. The public will grow tired.

PEREZ NOTE

Angelina and Brad—the soccer

team will be complete once they have fifteen kids. Game over. Hopefully, Angelina will start speaking to her dad, and Brad will call Jen, and they'll have coffee. Then the whole world would really be saved!

Katie Holmes and Tom Cruise—

if they want to continue being the freaks that they are, then they are perfect for each other. Until the alien spaceship comes back down to grab them and take them back to the homeland, I guess we are stuck with them. Suri's a good kid, and I think they mean well. They just have a weird way of going about everything they do. I have two big questions for this relationship, though. Will they ever just relax and be normal? And will Katie's career ever *really* take off?

Victoria and David Beckham—maybe Becks could coach Brangelina's soccer team? I don't see how he could really be satisfied with Posh for all eternity. He should marry someone who smiles once in a while.

Oprah—she and Gayle will finally make a commitment to each another. Stedman rejoices!

Madonna—she'll get together with another younger athlete. When she's eighty, she'll be banging a sixty-year-old golfer to stay young!

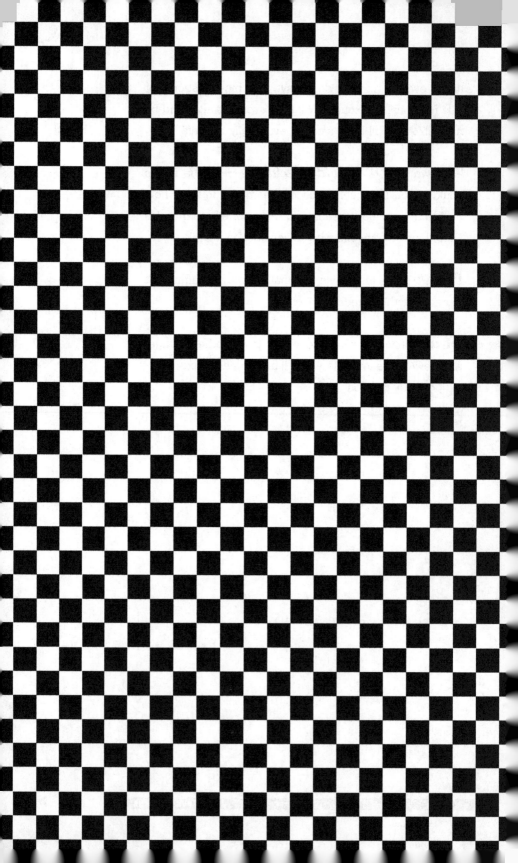

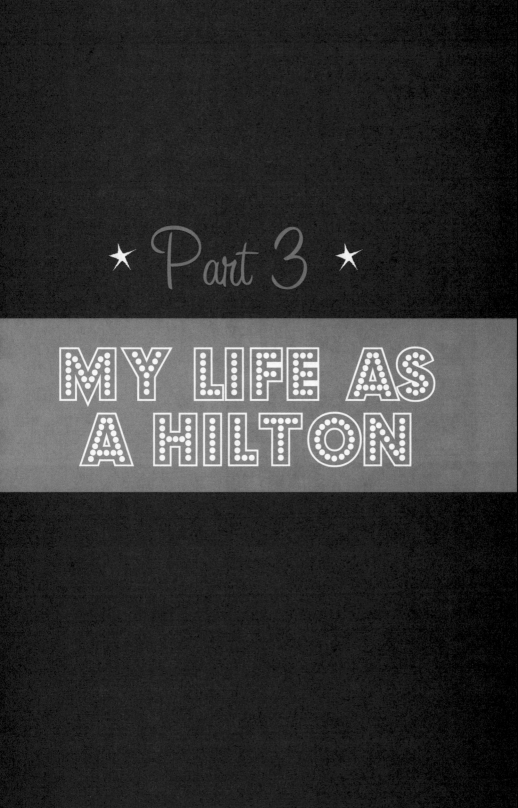

Part 3

MY LIFE AS A HILTON

the gossip game

I started my Web site as a fun way to write about gossip and entertainment. The longer I did it, and the more readers I got, the more tipsters and regular people started sending me items that they saw. When I go to parties, people recognize me, and that's another contact in my bag of tricks. I don't have a publicist walking me around to introduce me to people, I just do it myself. The most important part of gathering dirt is getting fresh contacts and maintaining them.

I don't just get just one tip on where a celebrity is; I get ten. If Jessica Simpson and Tony Romo are having lunch in Dallas, Texas, I not only get tips from readers saying, "I just saw Tony and Jessica at Sushi Samba! They were holding hands." I also get cell phone pictures, times, dates, and sometimes even an on-the-record quote from the tipster. And I don't even have to leave my computer!

Now, I'm not going to just post something that a random reader sends in. She could be a crackhead! But when many different readers start sending me e-mails about the same sighting, I start to believe it. When I've got random people telling me they saw the same thing, then I'm pretty confident it happened. Even then, I'm a little suspicious, so I dig around more. You can't just blindly post an item someone sends you. There are a lot of crackheads out there who send me crazy tips—a

Everyone loves to gossip . . .

lot of them false or, worse, concerning boring celebrities whom I don't care about.

Ultimately, my best sources are my friends. They don't lie, they don't have hidden agendas—they've just got information, and they want to share it.

When you put it out there that you want items, people start sending them to you. Everyone loves to gossip, and in an era of cell phones and digital cameras and e-mail and texting, it's virtually impossible for a celebrity to walk down the street or into a restaurant without being noticed by somebody. My readers are so important to me, because they let me know who is where. Sometimes it's fake—but when I see ten e-mails coming in my in-box telling me that Lance Armstrong and Kate Hudson have been spotted hooking up at a bar in Texas, I know it's true. So I check it out. You always have to check out your tips and sources. You can't just print what someone tells you. You've got to ask around. I would say 75 percent of the stuff I get e-mailed to me is true. I get around three hundred tips a day from readers and regulars. I need to make about forty posts a day—so keep 'em coming! There's never a lack of information, so it's just a matter of what you find interesting.

> My readers are so important to me, because they let me know who is where.

A lot of what I do on my Web site is to get people talking and get them involved. Sometimes there's no *real* story, but there's just a hunch or observation that I notice. For instance, sometimes people like Nick Lachey and Vanessa Minnillo will go out partying separately several nights of the week. Maybe they're still together. Maybe they've split. We're simply saying we rarely see them hanging out together. There's no right or wrong way to cover it, so I'll just say, "We haven't seen them together in a while—do you think they are okay?" You have the opportunity to leave comments, click on things, and vote. That's a level of interactivity that only the Web can offer, and it's a great way to engage my readers and make it a shared experience.

Confirmations have become superimportant in the world of gossip. This is basically when a publicist or spokesperson for a celebrity confirms (on or off the record) that an event or occurrence did take place. A split, a divorce, a birth, an incident, an engagement, or a pregnancy—confirmations are definitely important. But you can't always get a publicist to confirm things. So most important is just getting the item first. A perfect example was the R. Kelly trial in June of 2008. I was hitting F5 on all of the Chicago news Web sites, watching TV reports—I wanted that story the second it hit, so I could link it. The best example was when Kate Hudson and Lance Armstrong first got together. It was almost summertime in 2008, and for the most part everyone still thought Kate was with Owen Wilson. Just a week or so earlier, they had been spotted together! But I randomly started getting these tips on my e-mail that Kate was being spotted in Texas with Lance Armstrong! At first I didn't believe it, but then I got a second e-mail, and a third e-mail. Pretty soon, I had about a dozen e-mails from various people saying they saw Kate and Lance . . . together! So I made a couple of calls to people who would be able to confirm that the two of them were together, and sure enough, it was true! I not only had confirmation they were newly seeing each other, but I had times, places, and dates of places they had been together! The world had let me know.

I'm not a traditional journalist, but I do respect the codes of the trade. I never reveal sources, no matter what. You have to keep secrets, or no one will ever want to talk to you. Even when you get drunk, you've got to be a locked vault! I wish I could do more actual reporting, but that takes time. I wish I could call up the police or get comments from official spokespeople every time there is breaking news or drama. Ideally, that's what I'd do in the future. I'd love to have more staff, hire reporters, and run a news department for PerezHilton.com!

I'm just one person, but the paparazzi and the gossip mags are teams of hundreds all hunting for the latest breaking news. I don't think Brad and Angelina have ever been off the radar for more than four or five days since getting together. They'll have disappeared for a few days, and then magically a photographer catches Brad zipping through downtown LA on his Ducati bike. They can't hide! I've always thought it was puzzling that the American government can never find the terrorists they're looking for or that the police can't always find the murderer. What they need to do is employ gossip reporters, because gossip reporters can find out anything! Tom and Katie can go unseen for days at a time, but then they magically appear on the other side of the world, even when they are trying to hide. Gossip is all about staying on top of the story, building sources, maintaining them, and then breaking the news before anyone else.

tipsters and trading

There are really only two ways to get gossip. The first is tipsters, and the second is favors from someone "in the know." Virtually all people in the know want something in return. It doesn't have to be immediate, but nothing comes for free. At some point, they will want a favor in return, and that's fine. Everyone has a job and an agenda. Luckily for me, I'm doing things on my own terms, so I don't have to answer to anyone.

Let's say I get a tip, but I don't have the resources or the means to follow it up or push it forward. I'll give it to a friend who works at a magazine. Maybe he can do something better with it. Sometimes I'd like something in return, sometimes not. Gossip comes down to trading: What are you going to get in return for what you did for somebody? Hey, this is work, and nothing comes for free!

The same publicists who represent some of the biggest celebrities in Hollywood also happen to represent hotels, skin-care products, fashion lines, stores, restaurants, car companies, jewelry, and charities. As a celebrity journalist, if you mention the publicist's cellulite-fighting cream, they might just tell you a little dirt on one of their clients. Or maybe they'll just tip you off as to where their client is going for dinner, or what town they happen to be visiting. Just a little dirt to keep everyone happy. That's a very common practice. Publicists do that all the time. Especially publicists who coordinate events. "If you mention this product, I will tell you this and that."

Sometimes they exaggerate or fudge the truth, and they do whatever it takes to get their products mentioned. For instance, if a publicist is throwing a huge party at a club sponsored by a major liquor company, that publicist will do everything in her power to dig up a gossip item to make the party worth mentioning in your column the next day. (As long as you promise to mention the club and the liquor sponsor, they'll practically write up the whole gossip item for you!) I wonder if the celebrities are aware this is going on?

A publicist will sometimes trade their C-list client for an A-list client. Basically, if you promise to mention their C-list client in your gossip pages, they will in exchange provide you with a good item about or access to their A-list client. It's all part of the gossip game!

There's also the practice of "killing an item." This happens a lot, but not by me! This is where the magazines that most need to cater to the publicists and be friendly to celebrities actually kill items that may be hurtful (no matter how true). I don't give a fuck about publicists. I don't need access to their clients, and I don't have to keep them happy. I will rarely kill an item, because all gossip items were created equal! They are an inalienable right.

gossip reporters can find out anything!

celebrities as sources

Some of the most well-connected people in Hollywood are the celebrities themselves. No one has better gossip than a celebrity. Whether it's a former friend, a current friend, a costar, a bitter sibling, an enemy, or an ex-lover, celebrities have the best dirt out there.

Not all of them are talkers—most celebrities are well trained in keeping things secret. But some celebrities just can't help themselves, and they are a wealth of gossip information! You gotta be very careful, though—you don't want to seem like a desperate reporter trying to get info. You want to befriend them and fit in, just have fun! Stuff will come of it eventually. Some celebrities talk right off the bat. But if they don't, I never try to pull info out of a celebrity. I never ask people for info. Unless it's something big, in which case I'll say, "I never do this, but . . ." You don't want to develop a reputation for talking to people only to get information. Over the years, I've befriended a number of good celebrity sources, people whom I trust and who trust me. At this point, I would say I rely heavily and consistently on ten good celebrities who give me a good story at least once a month.

> No one has better gossip than a celebrity.

celebrities who tip off the paparazzi

Charlie Sheen sold his exclusive wedding shots to *OK!* magazine, but what about the honeymoon shots? Conveniently, one photo agency got them and sold them to all of the other magazines. Just a few shots, though, of Charlie and Brooke Mueller "honeymooning privately." I'm sure they got a cut of the money. Hey, anyone who sells his wedding photos, you never know what he is capable of!

Denise Richards does it all the time. It's been reported that she would invite paparazzi into her gated community and onto the playground to shoot photos of her playing with her two children. It was upsetting to all of the people living in the community. She's been pimping out those girls forever now. Only recently have people been catching on. She's been whoring them out practically since they were born, poor kids. They will grow up like Rumer Willis, famous kids with famous parents who have no drive to do anything other than be famous. They'll probably grow up saying, "If Rumer can do it, I can do it! I'm not as ugly or untalented!"

Heidi and Spencer *call their own paparazzi. They are about as real as the reality show they are on.* They call a photo agency called Pacific Coast News (PCN). It's so blatantly obvious—if you go to Pacific Coast News's Web site and browse "Heidi Montag and Spencer Pratt," you will see tons of photos of Heidi and Spencer in Mexico! Heidi and Spencer on the beach! Heidi and Spencer go flower shopping! Kudos to them—it actually raised their profile immensely; they even passed their costar and nemesis L.C. It makes them a lot of money, because they split the profits from the photo agency.What's so crazy is that now it's gotten to a point where the audience is catching on, and no one cares!

A lot of times, Lindsay Lohan gets cash for her paparazzi photos. She'll go into a store or a restaurant, and "conveniently" a photographer gets a few shots. It's actually smart of her. She knows the paparazzi are going to get her anyway, so why not make a profit from it? But Lindsay also loves the attention, and she wouldn't know what to do with herself if one day she stepped out of her house and no photogs were there to chase her!

No one cares about Kristin Cavallari anymore, so she has to resort to fake paparazzi shots. "Oh, no! I got a parking ticket!" "Look at me, I'm eating ice cream!"

There was a time during her major meltdown in 2007 that Britney Spears was tipping off tons of photographers. She had thirty of them trailing her practically every day! She used to call the agency X17 and invite them into her home to party! And her pal, that Sam Lutfi character, was totally in bed with the photogs and swinging deals as well.

Once in a while, Brad and Angelina tip off everyone. I don't think *they* personally do it. I think it's more people in their camp, but they're aware of it. I mean, they sell their baby photos every chance they get. So there's proof right there that they deal with photographers. But I became suspicious about them after they first hooked up on the beach in Kenya. The *very* first photo of them didn't arrive in the in-box of photo editors until *after* they had left the country. As if Angelina had given them strict orders to take the photo (the first ever of Brad and Angelina together, on the other side of the world!) but not send it out for sale until she had left the country—so no one else could tag along and try to get new photos.

Mario Lopez is always looking buff on the beach, showing off his biceps and abs—always looking hot and studly. I don't know if he is in cahoots with the paparazzi, but he puts himself out there and is never caught off guard.

Mischa Barton totally works with Pacific Coast News. PCN is on the forefront of being in bed with celebs. They work with Andy Baldwin, Heidi and Spencer, Brittny Gastineau, Mischa, Marla Maples, lots of the *Bachelor* and *Bachelorette* people—basically anyone who needs press. I've even prearranged PCN photos! With Mischa, they always take flattering photos. Regular, non-PCN photos show her with cellulite and looking less than glamorous—but PCN shots show her looking fabulous! Can you say Photoshop?

Paris Hilton doesn't do it as much anymore, but back in the day, she used to always tip off the paparazzi. Now it's just every once in a while. She's constantly hawking a new product or new style, and she needs to be seen with it so she gets that endorsement money.

No one cares about Kristin Cavallari anymore, so she has to resort to fake paparazzi shots.

the best unconfirmed rumors that i wish were true

Sometimes a rumor is better than the truth. Sometimes it's better to have the public think you are gay, an addict, sick, or insane, just so there will be some interest in you. If they knew that six nights a week you actually just sat home and smoked weed from your vaporizer before your masseuse came over and rubbed you down before bed, they'd probably be pretty bored with you. If all hiltons did that, then no one would buy gossip magazines or log on to my site. I'd be out of a job! Or actually, I'd have to get one!

The best thing that can happen is to have everyone talking about you. It's a hell of a lot better than having no one talking about you. You don't want to be forgotten in Hollywood. Getting work is all about buzz—and if you've got no buzz, you've got nada! So even if it's all lies and unkind things, at least they are focusing on you. Sometimes it's better to let the rumor exist. Who gives a shit if people are talking trash about you—they'll rarely do it to your face! So fuck 'em! Bring on the rumors. Ultimately, it depends on how hurtful they are to you. Then you can decide whether or not to set the record straight. Maybe you want to, or maybe the rumor is so good and salacious that you're better off letting it persist. I personally don't think any unconfirmed rumor, whether it's positive or negative, hurts your career. Like they say, any press is good press. I don't think Brad and Angelina have suffered from all of the negative tabloid press they've been given over the years. How could they have—they are the biggest stars on the planet! And even if you fuck up, Hollywood is a very forgiving industry. Paris Hilton is just as big now as she ever was. No matter how many times she goes to jail or how many guys she dates, she'll always be "Paris Hilton"!

The fact is that the thought of what a celebrity does is 90 percent better than what they actually do. And yeah, while a lot of hiltons are swinging from the chandeliers and doing backflips in the beds of some of the hottest people on the planet, a lot of them are workaholics, just like you and me. They go from the gym to the movie set to dinner to home and back to the gym and movie set and dinner the next day, sometimes twelve months out of the year. Same boring schedule, same mundane life. Work, work, work.

Of course, those are just the stiff-asses. Fortunately, a lot of celebrities *do* participate in crazy things. A lot of them *are* secretly gay. A lot them actually *do* massive amounts of drugs. Most of things written about hiltons actually *are* true. You couldn't even make up the story that Nicole Richie took some pills and drove the wrong way down a major freeway. She did it all on her own, without the help of tabloids, publicists, or rumors. That was a reality moment. Paris did go to jail. Brad did leave Jen and go with Angelina, Jen didn't recover, Angelina did rack up six kids and counting, and she did become the most famous female celebrity on the planet. Shit really happens, so we don't have to make everything up. But truths will always leave a little room for rumors and myths and fables. Not everything we read, hear,

One of my favorite rumors of all time is the rumor that Tom Cruise is gay.

What do you think of the rumor that Suri is made from the sperm of Scientology's creator, L. Ron Hubbard?

or see is true, because Hollywood does create a lot of rumors, some of which get repeated year after year. I wish a lot of them were true; it sure would make things a lot more interesting. But despite what's been said, I feel like most of the rumors just don't pan out, and I'm happy to put a lot of them to bed.

One of my favorite rumors of all time is the rumor that Tom Cruise is gay. At this point, I don't even want him to be gay. I'd rather him be freaky and asexual. I don't want him on my team, and the straights don't want him on their team. He can be on his own team—in his own league, for that matter. There are all of these crazy rumors that he auditioned people for the role of his wife and that Katie Holmes won out. I don't think they are true, but they're out there. He's a weird guy, but if he were gay, someone would have come forward by now and sold his story! Because no one ever has, it leads me to think he's either straight (he is married with a kid, after all!) or just asexual (since no one has come forward saying otherwise).

Even though I don't want Tom to be gay, I hope the rumor is true that Tom Cruise was caught in bed with Rob Thomas! That one came out of nowhere . . . Rob and Tom, WTF? In 2005, a rumor surfaced that these two were caught in bed together, and that Rob's wife, Marisol, was ready to expose the whole thing. So Tom quickly got together with Katie Holmes and pres-to—bye-bye, gay rumors! I don't think it's true, but it sure is an awesome rumor. Rob obviously saw the humor in the rumor, and he said his wife didn't mind. "As long as I sleep with A-list celebrities, I'm completely OK," Rob joked. "All my gay friends love it. They all say, 'Our friends love you even more now!'"

Of course, there's also that rumor that Tom is controlling Katie. While this is just a rumor . . . I totally believe it! Looking at her body language, her eyes, her words, the fact that she cut off her old friends—it certainly doesn't seem like she's happy and doing everything she wants. Maybe she is; maybe she isn't. That's why this is just a rumor. But I can totally believe rumors if I want! And I believe this one. It doesn't make it true, but everything from the way he holds her (he always grabs her by the wrist and pulls and tugs at her) to the way she *totally* changed since being with him—everything makes me think he's controlling her. What do you think?

What do you think of the rumor that Suri is made from the sperm of Scientology's creator, L. Ron Hubbard? I think maybe. I do find it suspicious that Nicole Kidman and Tom Cruise couldn't have a kid for ten years; then all of a sudden Katie was pregnant. Was it a prosthetic bump? The whole pregnancy was under suspicion. Something weird going on there, for sure!

Is John Travolta gay? Another great rumor, right? I think that one is true! I heard a rumor that a particular actor was propositioned by him once. This actor used to be a model and

Like they say, any press is good press.

was working on the same set, and John was trying to go into his trailer and get it on with him—like, all of the time! The guy wasn't into it, but John kept persisting. The guy finally videotaped John trying to seduce him, and then he allegedly blackmailed John for a lot of money. A celebrity told me this, so I believe it! Sure, he's married to Kelly Preston, but she's a nobody who married him so she doesn't have to work. And she's drinking the Scientology juice, just like Katie Holmes!

There's the "Jamie Lee Curtis is a hermaphrodite" rumor. I think that might be true! She doesn't look overtly male or masculine, so it's kind of an insult. But the rumor's out there. . . . I don't know, she's always had short hair.

In the summer of 2008, I wrote about a rumor concerning Chace Crawford and Ed Westwick from *Gossip Girl*. Something fishy was going on! I had been contacted by entertainment reporters from the *New York Post* and the *New York Daily News*—within days of each other. They both wanted to share a piece of info too juicy to print, they said. Seemed like on-set sources, which the pubs told us were reliable, reported to each paper that Chace Crawford and *Gossip Girl* costar and real-life roommate Ed Westwick were in a relationship and not trying to hide it, at least on set. Both NY papers told us that Chace and Ed were seen kissing, openmouthed, in Chace's trailer. I don't know if it was true or not, but it was very interesting! The *Post* and *Daily News* both declined to publish this item, because

There's the "Jamie Lee Curtis is a hermaphrodite" rumor. I think that might be true!

they don't like to "out" people. Well, it's either true or someone is trying to spread rumors to both New York papers about the *Gossip Girl* costars. I was happy to put it out there, because we hope it's true—they'd be a hot couple! Of course, don't forget that celebrities are *very* aware of rumors written about them. Just days later, Ed Westwick celebrated his twenty-first birthday at TAO in Las Vegas. His very good friend and real-life roommate, Chace Crawford, was supposed to be there. Unfortunately, Chace canceled at the last minute (a day before). Geesh, *what* could have caused him to cancel?

There's the rumor that Brad cheated on Jen Aniston with Angelina. I've said repeatedly that no, I don't think so. I don't think it happened. I think that marriage was over before Brad and Angelina got together. I don't think in this world of gossip and tabloids and paparazzi that if you are Brad Pitt, you can get away with cheating. Did he flirt with Angelina on set? Maybe. Was Jen's not wanting to have kids the reason Brad left? Most likely. All of the math came together for a perfect equation . . . the greatest gossip story ever.

What about the rumor that Scarlett Johansson banged Benicio Del Toro in a Chateau Marmont hotel elevator after the 2004 Oscars? That would be great if it were true! This is a perfect example of a star understanding the power of a rumor. Benicio hinted that he really did have sex with Scarlett in an elevator. Scarlett was new to the gossip scene at that point, and she played it off like it was a bad rumor. She denied the tryst, saying, "I went home alone that night to my mom's house, but nobody cares about that. It was so embarrassing. I felt horrible about the way that portrayed Benicio." But he didn't seem to mind! Benicio played it up like a true veteran. He actually all

I love the one that says the kid from *The Wonder Years* grew up and became Marilyn Manson. Ha!

but confirmed it in a 2005 interview with *Esquire* magazine. He said, "Did I ever have sex in an elevator with Scarlett Johansson after an awards show? I kind of, like, you know, I, well. I don't know. Let's leave that to somebody's imagination. Let's not promote it. I'm sure it has happened before. It might not be the last time either." By doing that, Benicio totally secured his place in the Rumors Hall of Fame! It's a great one! Had he denied it, the item probably would have died a quick death. But he didn't, so it lives on!

I don't think the Richard Gere gerbil rumor is true. Here's this great rumor about a hot A-list actor sticking a gerbil up his ass for pleasure . . . and having to go to the hospital to get it removed. Of course, he's never addressed it. Why not just come out and say, "No, it's not true," even if it was? Seems weird he's never denied it or spoken about it. Maybe he's waiting until the perfect moment, when he's got a movie coming out and he's nominated for an Oscar and he wants to make a big buzz. He could claim it's true to Barbara Walters or Diane Sawyer, and the buzz would be huge!

There have been a ton of rumors out there that Jen Aniston is a huge stoner. But you know what? Jen Aniston's lawyers like to sue if you talk about her alleged pot smoking! So I'm not going to talk about Jen Aniston's alleged pot smoking! Because they'll sue me if I say Jen Aniston allegedly smokes pot! So you won't hear me mentioning anything about Jen Aniston and pot in the same sentence, because I don't want to get sued. They have sued before, you know, when someone tried to allege that she smoked pot.

I think Lauren Conrad's sex tape with ex-boyfriend Jason Wahler is true for sure. After all, I broke that story! I don't know if it's actual sex, but there's definitely something that was going on. Maybe BJs aren't considered sex anymore? Maybe it's not full penetration, but the rumor says that there is some video out there with something on it that L.C. does *not* want you to see.

Madonna and Guy are a perfect example of rumors heating up to the point to which, where there's smoke, there's fire. The rumor of their split always had some truth to it. It's like the Madonna lesbian rumors; I think there is some truth to those, too. Madonna lives her life her way. For months if not years, Madonna and Guy were rocked by rumors; then in the summer of 2008, a lot of it came to a head. At some point, *rumors are true.* They just get twisted around somewhat.

I love the one that says the kid from *The Wonder Years* grew up and became Marilyn Manson. Ha! Manson was not on *The Wonder Years.* It was Josh Saviano, who grew up to be a lawyer. What would you rather have, people thinking you're a boring lawyer or a satanic rock star? Even "Paul" knew the power of a good rumor! But it's not true.

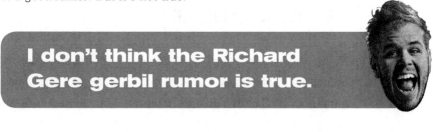

I don't think the Richard Gere gerbil rumor is true.

There were all of these rumors that Angelina and her brother, James Haven, used to hook up. Not true . . . come on! I would be shocked if this were true. I don't think she's that weird. It all started with a quote Angelina made at the 2000 Oscars, when she said, "I'm so in love with my brother right now," and they shared a long kiss on the lips. Angelina said, "I don't know if it's divorced families, but he and I were each other's everything. We've always been best friends. He's the funniest, sweetest person I know. He just gives me so much love, it's great." Haven then said: "It's a very weird thing when a brother and sister can't show love for each other in public without people gossiping about them." Yeah, well . . . people turn it into more than it was, though. She was probably drunk or high when she was babbling like that. It's not like she was thinking rationally. If you asked her now, "Were you drunk or high when you said those things," she might answer yes!

I believe the rumor that Oprah and Gayle are lesbians. The fact that Oprah and Gayle King have been *such* close friends is a little odd. I mean, how come we don't ever hear about her other friends? Does she have only *one* good friend? And Oprah's a little too good to her. She puts Gayle's kids through school, buys her homes, made her famous, gave her a TV show (which failed). She just does a lot for her. Stedman may be okay with it . . . I don't know. It all just seems odd!

celebrity run-ins

Doing this job has led to some pretty interesting run-ins. Sometimes I find myself making out with John Mayer at four a.m. in an NYC club (while his then-girlfriend Jessica rubs his cock!), and sometimes I feel like my life is being threatened. It's the complete spectrum! I take the good with the bad. When I run into someone whom I am not so nice to on the Web site, I try to avoid them, but a lot of times they try to confront me. Hiltons aren't used to being picked on. A hilton goes after what they want and they attack, attack, attack. They have nothing better to do than to Google themselves and check out my site all day to see if I wrote about them. And when I do, it pisses them off. So in public, they either run in the other direction, or they come straight at me. I dish it, so I have to take it. The ones who have a sense of humor and don't scream at me? That's a real celebrity! Douche bags like Jesse Metcalfe? Loser!

Test Your Skill

Here's just a taste of what some celebrities have said to me. Try to match the quote to the celebrity below:

1. "You say mean things about me."

2. "I go on your Web site every day."

3. "Stop writing trash about me."

4. "Do you know how many times I've fantasized about killing you?"

5. "Do I really have 'zombie hands'?"

6. "You've just been especially mean to me and it hurts."

A. Jesse Metcalfe

B. Paris Hilton

C. Nicole Richie

D. Avril Lavigne

E. Lindsay Lohan

F. Tara Reid

Answer key: 1 B, 2 E, 3 F, 4 A, 5 C, 6 D

There was a time when I was treated like a freak/outsider and banned from the hot party hotel the Chateau Marmont and the Hollywood club du jour, Hyde, out of fear that I would write something about the celebrities partying inside. They didn't want me there, so fuck 'em—I wouldn't go. Hyde died down soon enough. It's so stupid that Hollywood wants privacy, yet instead of partying in unannounced places, they all go to the same five clubs and have lunch at the Ivy. Want to know where a celebrity is going to be on a Tuesday night? You don't have to be Perez Hilton—young Hollywood is on a schedule now, and everyone knows it. Everyone knows that Monday-night parties are at one place, Tuesday-night parties are at another . . . and so on. In New York, it's always about Butter Mondays. It's been that way for years. The year 2008 brought Teddy's on Thursdays in LA. Why would I want to try to get into these places now? It would be humiliating if I couldn't get in. I haven't done anything crazy like a Courtney Love to be banned from Chateau—but they probably wouldn't let me in. Maybe I still go, in disguise . . . and they just don't know it.

I have made a lot of friends along the way, and I've made a few enemies. I can't say I'm always the nicest person to Madonna, but when her "best friend," Ingrid Casares, saw me at a Madonna concert once, she handed me front-row tickets. That bought Madonna at least a few months of good coverage on my site—until she stole that boy from Africa! So not all moments with celebrities are bad. I call a lot of celebrities friends, and I get along with a lot of Hollywood: Selma Blair, Tori Spelling, Jewel, Heidi Montag, Spencer Pratt, Paris, Amanda Bynes, Mika. Musicians are cool with me; they know I love music. Anne Hathaway gave me a shout-out once on *TRL,* and I've never even met her! Eva Mendes gave me a shout-out in an

interview, and I've never met her either—but I'd like to; she's a fellow Cubana!

On the opposite end of the spectrum are times like when I was elbowed in the face at a club by a friend of Nicole Richie's, Andy LeCompte—he's a fucking hairdresser who wants to be famous. He was dancing on a banquette (annoying move number 1!), and he just elbowed me in my face "accidentally." He was like, "You are rude." I'm like, "Excuse me; you just elbowed me in the face!" He was very obnoxious about it, and he claimed he didn't see me. But he did the same thing to Paris Hilton. He was doing the running man at Teddy's in LA, and he kicked Paris. It's a cheap and easy move. Lame.

I first met Paris Hilton in September during Fashion Week many, many years ago. I went up to her and said, "Listen, I've just got to tell you that I named my Web site as an homage to you." I was this gushing, gay fanboy. She said, "You say mean things about me." And I was like, "No, no, no. I love you. If I didn't care about you, I wouldn't talk about you." At first, she hated me, but she got to know me, and we soon became friends. I saw her in Vegas shortly after I met her. She had just called off her engagement to Paris Latsis, and she talked to me on the red carpet at an event. When she stopped to talk to me, every other reporter was looking at me like, "Who is that guy? Why is she only talking to him?" Before I had met Paris, I had pagesixsixsix.com, so she didn't make me, but being associated with her gave me some reflected glory.

> Hollywood wants privacy, yet instead of partying in unannounced places, they all go to the same five clubs.

I met Lindsay at Usher's birthday party a few years back. She told me, "I go on your Web site every day." But that was before she was Lindsay Blohan. I'll give it to her: *Mean Girls* was a success, but what has she done since then? She's like the redhead version of Tara Reid. *Herbie Fully Loaded* bombed; so did *Just My Luck*. *A Prairie Home Companion* tanked (no one even talked about her performance), and her role in *Bobby* was minuscule and overshadowed. She's been in trouble so much with the law and in the public eye that producers don't even want her in their movies, because you never know if she'll actually show up! When Lindsay was being ridiculed by Morgan Creek Productions CEO James G. Robinson (Lindsay had been showing up to work late every day on the set of her film *Georgia Rule*, and Robinson had issued a letter to the press stating that Lindsay was immature and threatening the profitability of the film), she all of a sudden was under a lot of heat. Hollywood was watching her as if she were done. Everyone wanted to know what her next move was. But Lindsay didn't fire back by appearing on CNN's *Larry King Live* or talking to Leno or Couric. Nope. Instead, she waltzed into my office at that time, the Coffee Bean on Sunset, and ordered a latte to go. Of course, while there, she came over to me and said hello, then told me she was "going to be twenty minutes early" to the set of her movie that day. Remember, that was after days of missing work and being late. To show up twenty minutes early for her was like a new beginning. Her missing work and Robinson's issuing that letter were the story of the moment in Hollywood. Anyway, a lot of people read my site, and her fans come to me for info. That was a great moment. She knew to come directly to me, so I'd put it out there that she was making a concerted effort to change. And ten minutes later, the whole world knew the scoop as I pressed the button to post it on my site. Choreographed or not, the drop-in resulted in a nice hit of good press for Lohan that didn't require her to sit down for a laborious, self-flagellating interview. Within minutes, I had posted a note about the incident on my Web site: "We've been showing her some tough love lately, but Lindsay Lohan is getting her act together . . . Keep it up, LL!" And that was that. She was the ultimate hilton that day. She worked the media, did her job, and went home. For that moment, she was on her game.

When I first started blogging, I took F-lister Tara Reid and called her out on what she is: "Tired Reid." I put up unflattering paparazzi photos of her all over my site. She obviously wasn't so thrilled. While most gossip magazines leave Tara out of their publication because she doesn't do anything and no one cares, I decided to include her on my Web site for those same reasons. It all started when I mocked Tara's thirtieth birthday party (I called it her fortieth) and flat-out embarrassed her in her every attempt to be a celebrity. She's lame—she should just give it up and get a bartending job! It was at this point that I had one of my first (but certainly not my last) encounters with an angry celebrity. As with all great Hollywood dramas, this one was beautifully lit and couldn't have taken place at a more cinematic location: poolside at a fabulous hotel. It was late spring at the Roosevelt Hotel, a place where all of the stars go to hang. I was attending a birthday party with my good friend, inspiration, and faux cousin Paris Hilton. An angry Reid appeared out of nowhere, came over to me, and demanded that I refrain from writing about her on my site. She just couldn't take it anymore. She tried to get me kicked out of the party. Paris vouched for me and took my side—letting me stay. It was such unnecessary drama. She was totally on something that night! "Frequent bathroom trips." She stared me down and said, "Stop writing trash about me." So I said, "Stop reading my Web site." "Stop writing trash about me." "Stop reading my Web site." "Stop writing trash about me." "Stop reading my Web site." This went on literally for, like, three minutes. Then she said she'd throw me in the pool. In retrospect, I wish she had. At the time, I didn't want her to (I had my camera and phone on me). But looking back, that would have been amazing.

Anyone who reads my site knows that's the wrong way to get me to lay off. Send me a brand-new Prada suit? Maybe. A lifetime supply of Pinkberry ice cream? Sure. But attack me in public and order me around? That's just going to turn me into an angry pit bull. Real celebrities like Angelina Jolie don't have time for petty stuff like that. But this beyotch Tara is famous for being famous. Her movies flop, her TV shows get canceled, and yet everyone knows who Tara Reid is. Her titty popped out while she was on the red carpet of Diddy's birthday bash, and the whole world saw her overexposed, deformed, plastic surgery–ridden nipple. This girl would have been long forgotten if not for that moment, and the countless number of times we've seen her hammered stumbling out of a club. I pick on her a lot, but why not? I mean, what has she accomplished? It just goes to show that even an F-lister can have her fifteen minutes extended. After months and months of my picking on her, *Us Weekly* decided to talk to her about her botched plastic sur-

> While most gossip magazines leave Tara out of their publication because she doesn't do anything and no one cares, I decided to include her on my Web site for those same reasons.

gery—and it ended up being on their cover! They made a freak out of her, and she liked it! Because no matter how unflattering the topic, she got her "look at me" moment.

In December of '05, *Desperate Housewives* gardener Jesse Metcalfe sought me out at an LA nightclub, Les Deux—back when it was the place to go. He comes up to me and says, "How long is this going to go on for? Do you really think I am gay?" I am constantly calling Jesse gay and begging him to come out of the closet already. So I just said to him, "I think you are gay-ish." He responded with, "Dude, I'm not gay." Then he got close to me and said, "Do you know how many times I've fantasized about killing you?" I was a little bit shocked, to say the least. I didn't know what to say. He repeated it, as if I didn't hear him the first time. I haven't seen him since, fortunately. I can't say I had anything to do with his career tanking, because he had his own hand in ruining his career. He went to rehab and over-exposed himself.

Nicole Richie once strutted up to me at the Coffee Bean and asked me, "Do I really have 'zombie hands'?" And she demanded that I call her anorexic to her face. I had been ragging on Richie for months, saying the notoriously skinny star needed to eat a grain of rice, at least, if not a burger. I was showing pictures of her long, bony, zombie hands—a reader favorite. That was pretty ballsy of her to come up to me and say that, but she's a pretty ballsy girl. I didn't give in to her and say what she wanted me to say. I didn't say, "You aren't anorexic, and you don't have zombie hands." I was like, "Can't we just hug it out?" She had her gays with her, too, and I didn't want a scene caused at my place of work! I mean, she's a recovering heroin addict who has spent time in jail. She's not afraid to fuck a bitch up! I don't think she likes me, but I don't dislike her. If we knew each other better, I don't necessarily think we'd get along, but I also don't think we'd hate each other.

In March 2007, I went to a Christina Aguilera concert, and her people saw me in the crowd. They came up to me and said that Christina does this bit onstage during "Nasty Naughty Boy" where she invites someone onstage and ties them to a wheel and whips them. They asked me if I'd like to participate—and I'm like, "Yeah, I would love that! So cool!" She tied me to the wheel and said I was naughty and whipped me. Not like really whipped me, but like show-whipped me! It still hurt, though.

In July 2007, I was sitting at my laptop and I got a call from Avril Lavigne. She called me and asked if we could have a confidential phone conversation. I told her I wouldn't talk about it—but I did anyway. *Oops!* Apparently, she called the assistant of a mutual friend of ours and got my number that way. "I just wanted to reach out to you directly, instead of you hearing from my manager or publicist," she told me. Nice—I respect that. "I get what you do, but you've just been especially mean to me, and it hurts." She continued, "And I hear about it all the time. Journalists always ask me about you in interviews. You don't even know me!" How was I supposed to respond to something like that? I told her, "You just make it so easy sometimes." And she does make it easy. "I wish you would stop writing bad things about me," she said. My heart kinda sank. I felt really bad for her. Then I remembered: She's a douche! She needs to stop being such a hack, and then maybe I will be nice.

AFTERWORD

Dear Mr. Warhol,

You once described yourself as someone who'd like to sit home and watch every party that he's invited to on a monitor in his bedroom. I often feel the same way, and you could say that I've built a career out of doing exactly that. You created the blueprint in so many ways, and I couldn't help but model myself after you. Like, I'll always deny that I'm a real celebrity, because I feel like an outsider who subjugates himself before the truly famous. I know you felt the same way when you painted Marilyn Monroe and Elizabeth Taylor. You switched from painting to silk screen to downplay your own role in the production of your work, and you mass-produced your art and worked with collaborators, all because you wanted to disappear from the process. It wasn't because you didn't love glamour; you loved it more than anyone, like I do. You were just shy, and you wanted to be invisible as you watched, like viewing a monitor from your bedroom. The monitor I watch is on my laptop, and my bedroom is my bedroom, or sometimes the Coffee Bean.

But the funny thing about silk screens, the thing you loved about them, was mass production. You celebrated Campbell's soup and Coca-Cola because they were mass-produced, but your sincerest flattery was imitation—by using silk screens, you mass-produced your paintings of mass-produced subjects. And when you inspired Perez Hilton, you didn't create a painting, Andy; you created a silk screen! Every post I make is reproduced on the monitor of every person who visits PerezHilton.com, and every reader becomes a reproduction of you and me—imagine millions of people sitting in their bedrooms in front of monitors, watching not only the parties they were invited to, but especially the parties they'll never be invited to. They are loving glamour, loving Hollywood, loving plastic, and wanting to be plastic . . . *just like us!* You created a space in the world that you didn't have growing up in working-class Pittsburgh, gay and with immigrant parents. A space for people who love the lowbrow, the frivolous, the mundane, the shallow, the crass, the common, the plastic, the marvelously tacky, and the horribly wonderful . . . people who could have just as easily gotten lost in the margins, like a Cuban gay boy with strangely colored hair, for example. I want to say thank you, Andy. We all do—all of us who watch the party from our bedrooms.

Love,
P.H.
2009

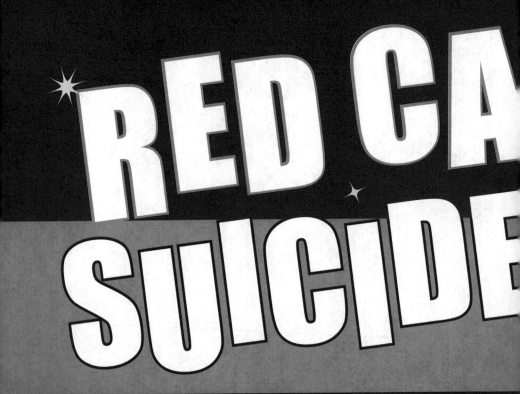

RED CA
SUICIDE

Laptop Samurai,
Gossip Gangstar, and the
Queen of All Media

PEREZ HILTON

With Jared Shapiro

a celebra book